"Honest to God and to her readers, Tania Bright gives head first into the most heartfelt issues of hope and human identity. Never scared to share the things that need to be said, nor those that go unsaid, she cuts to the chase and teaches us to reflect with 'kindsight'. Too often faith becomes the boxing glove we use to beat ourselves up. For those who feel battered, defeated, overwhelmed and diminished this book offers a much needed hand up."

– Dr Russell Rook

"If anyone was going to write this book it was going to be my great mate Tania. I've seen her refreshing honesty in action talking to a thousand men who gave her a standing ovation. I also know her when she's off the stage and she's exactly the same person. This book will warm your heart, help you to be kinder to yourself and to keep 'looking up' in hope and faith. Nice one, Tania. Your honesty and humility are compelling and personally challenging."

– Revd Carl Beech

"I love this book! A little bit manifesto, a lot of honesty – it's bold and beautiful about how to embrace life in all its rawness and fullness. Tania will help you re-think how to love yourself, and others, with the radical kindness Jesus demonstrates. Inspirational and completely unforgettable – I couldn't put it down."

– Rachel Gardner, founder of The Romance Academy

"Honesty is not for wimps, and neither is this book! Tania is a courageous and transparent warrior of hope-filled truth who takes us past polite conversation into the kind of honest discussion about tough issues that most of us long to have, but few of us actually experience. Every chapter reads like a coffee-fuelled chat with a fantastic friend – one moment raucous and a bit embarrassing, the next moment personal and poignant; but always compassionate and almost therapeutic in nature. This book is an incredibly practical and relevant resource that will greatly assist us all as we relate and minister to others, but also, I have no doubt that you, like me, will personally reflect on its content for some time. The benefit of 'kindsight' is, in every area of life, a powerful weapon for finding freedom. Pour yourself that coffee and get stuck in."

– **Cathy Madavan, Speaker, member of the Spring Harvest Planning Group and author of *Digging for Diamonds***

"Within the church, there are a number of topics that are often avoided, and a tendency not to admit that we are humans living imperfect lives and struggling with difficult times. No one could accuse Tania of this in this book, which mixes humour, insights, gentle challenges and a sense of support and encouragement as we learn from Tania's journey, and other voices that she has drawn upon! No one should finish reading this book feeling chastised, but rather have learned to practise 'kindsight': an ability to learn to be kind to ourselves (and others) in our past, present and future. Tania is an engaging public speaker, and this translates well into this book. Anyone who can get the word 'codswallop' naturally into a book, and recommends that 'it is better to eat a Mars Bar with good friends, than to eat broccoli alone' gets my vote!"

– **Bex Lewis**

"Tania is absolutely one of a kind, a breath of fresh air for the church today. She is one of those amazing people that after leaving her presence, you feel like you have spent time with Jesus. She lights up any room she walks in, not because of her charisma, but because of her deeply found confidence and trust in God that has come from an intimate walk with Him. Within these pages you will find her secret to the confident, abundant, Spirit-filled life that she so graciously carries everywhere she goes. Full of grace and truth, this book will take you to the heart of God and be ever so real about it along the journey. Thanks for being vulnerable and real, Tania… we desperately need it!"

– **Rob Peabody**

"This book is a generous gift. Tania has opened up her life and her heart to us in order to help us meet her God. I was hooked from the first page as Tania lets us into the sorrows and joys of her life story so far, showing us that even after some very dark times she has discovered the relentless grace of God. If you look back on your life and think 'if only…' Tania's concept of 'kindsight' will help you to see your past through the lens of the grace of God. She offers us a great gift. Make sure you don't miss out."

– Dr Krish Kandiah, President of London School of Theology and Founder of Home for Good

"Wow, a book that tells it as it is. If you hunger for reality and honesty, if you value relationships, you will love this book. Hindsight is the ability to reflect on an event or situation after it has happened whereas kindsight is the action and ability to stop, reflect and learn to be kind to yourself and to those involved. The world needs to not only know this word more but use it, as we are failing to tap into the most beautiful gift God has given us – love for each other and ourselves. When I first met Tania, we had chemistry, connection and instant commitment; observing and walking with her through some of the ups and downs has been a deep privilege. I highly recommend this book of wisdom and kindsight, but it does carry a health warning: your heart and life could be changed because of it."

– Vicky Taylor, founder of Free Range Chicks and Dignity, Leadership Consultant, Trainer and Coach

"Tania holds the heavy extremes of great strength and great vulnerability without fumbling over or dropping either. Her honesty and hard-won wisdom are life- and joy-giving. Long may she bless us by sharing them!"

– Abby Guinness, Event Director, Spring Harvest

"Tania writes as she speaks, and her strong and deliberate addressing of taboo subjects so personally will set the reader free of their religious spirit and/or their own personal struggles in these areas. Tania has such freedom in her own heart and it flows, nay, floods out of the book. It's time such a book was written by someone with the respect and value she has in the Christian world. Leave it to Tania to not just break through the barriers, but blow'm sky high.

"Her coining of the word 'kindsight' is nothing short of beautiful and the determination with which she practises what she preaches is a testimony to the power of the God she serves. Her love for people, friends, total strangers, and her two beautiful boys gives courage to those of us who look on as she journeys through life. If I could describe this book as just one thing, it would be HONEST. It is radically, freeingly, empoweringly, encouragingly, over the top honest and no reader can sit with it without being changed for the good, without wanting to know God more courageously and more deeply. This is a woman who knows the heart of God in a most beautiful way. I'm going to buy a dozen copies and give them away… captives can turn into mighty warriors; Tania is living proof."

– **Bev Murrill, Director, Christian Growth International**

"Well done for picking up this volume! This is an intensely practical, down-to-earth, life-researched book, which has been forged in some of the deepest and darkest experiences of life; Tania has been through them all and her dogged faith in the Lord Jesus to not only bring her through, but also to make something profoundly precious out of them, is the basis of the wisdom you will unearth as you read these chapters. I have had the privilege of seeing how Tania has tackled some of the things life has thrown at her and I have grown in profound admiration for her; she is a shining star and proof that what she writes about works. As you read this book you too will learn how to be kind to yourself as you work with the Holy Spirit to bring healing, wholeness and strength to your life."

– **Anne Coles, New Wine**

DON'T BEAT YOURSELF UP
Learning the wisdom of Kindsight

Tania Bright

MONARCH
BOOKS

Oxford UK, and Grand Rapids, USA

Published by Monarch Books
an imprint of
Lion Hudson plc
Wilkinson House, Jordan Hill Road, Oxford OX2 8DR, England
Email: monarch@lionhudson.com www.lionhudson.com/monarch

ISBN 978 0 85721 662 5
e-ISBN 978 0 85721 663 2

First edition 2015

Acknowledgments

Unless otherwise marked Scripture quotations are taken from the *Holy Bible, New
Living Translation*, copyright © 1996, 2004, 2007 by Tyndale House Foundation.
Used by permission of Tyndale House Publishers, Inc., Carol Stream, Illinois
60188. All rights reserved.

Scripture quotations marked AMP taken from the Amplified® Bible, Copyright ©
1954, 1958, 1962, 1965, 1987 by The Lockman Foundation. Used by permission.

Scripture quotation marked ESV is taken from The Holy Bible, English Standard
Version® (ESV®) copyright © 2001 by Crossway, a publishing ministry of Good
News Publishers. All rights reserved.

Extracts marked KJV are taken from The Authorized (King James) Version. Rights
in the Authorized Version are vested in the Crown. Reproduced by permission of
the Crown's patentee, Cambridge University Press.

Scripture quotations marked NIV are taken from the *Holy Bible, New International
Version*, copyright © 1973, 1978, 1984 International Bible Society. Used by
permission of Hodder & Stoughton, a member of the Hodder Headline Group. All
rights reserved. "NIV" is a trademark of International Bible Society. UK trademark
number 1448790.

Scripture quotations marked NKJV are taken from the New King James Version.
Copyright © 1982 by Thomas Nelson, Inc. Used by permission. All right reserved.

Further acknowledgments are on page 223.

A catalogue record for this book is available from the British Library

Printed and bound in the UK, July 2015, LH26

Contents

Acknowledgments

People have often asked me if I would pen something of the journey I've been on over the years. The task has always felt too gargantuan and my writing skills too clumsy, so I have never actioned it. Until Tony Collins laid the gauntlet down in front of me. He had belief in me and assumed I could write a book. That in itself was enough. And so I too believed in me and wrote a book. Thank you, Tony. I'd put the babies to bed, tidy the house, take a deep breath, and write late into the night: night after night, the words flowing until the story was told.

There've been cheerleaders on the way who have given me strength, made me laugh, and pushed me on; many of them are found in the pages ahead. They are part of my story. To my best friends Heidi and Ed, for their unswerving loyalty, fun and friendship. To my "special buddies"... to Russ, to Stella and Rob, to Katy and Phil, to Narn, to Joy, to Prince and Laura, to Victoria, to Katka, to Dr Laura, to Anna and Azariah, to the Dales' – life is richer with you all in it. I am blessed and grateful.

Thanks, too, for the wider friends who've provided wisdom and contribution: Jeff Lucas for his gracious foreword; Carl Beech for penning some well-crafted words for me; Tessa for your objective eye over the manuscript; Cathy Madavan for being a sisterly encourager; Vicky Taylor for sharp insights into my life; Anne Coles for being a constant mentor; Jenny Ward for being an inspirational and focused editor; and Rob and Medea Peabody for reading the first five pages once penned and being kind while offering direction!

And lastly, for my sons Mack and Charlie. Thank you, boys. You are joy-bringers. Funny, brave, and resilient. Every minute with you is a privilege. You have been the greatest gift I have ever received. I love you both. My prayer is that you don't cringe if ever you read this book: "Mum, why did you have to tell people that! You're so embarrassing!" Sons, I will do all I can to ensure you are kind to yourselves, that you live freely, and that you show yourselves and others compassion throughout your lives.

Foreword

It's a comment that my pal Adrian Plass has frequently made, usually accompanied by his wry but warm smile: "There's always a problem when truth is allowed to creep into Christianity." Sounds ridiculous, doesn't it? I can hear people huffing and puffing and making "disgusted of Woking" horsey noises, exhaling air through their indignantly flared nostrils at 500 psi.

I hear them protesting: "What are you blethering on about? Jesus is the truth, and so we are a people of the truth, aren't we?"

Yes. That is the theory. But the reality is often quite different. Christians, in common with the vast majority of the human race, frequently lie, hedge, exaggerate, pretend, and dance around the truth. This can happen when a question concerning how large a rear end looks in a pair of skinny jeans is proposed, prompting a lie in order to keep the peace. And in the church, there's often more hedging than is usually found at a garden centre when "difficult" subjects like self-image, pornography, masturbation, and guilt are mentioned. Much coughing can be heard from the cloisters. Although we *have* moved on a little. When I was a keen evangelical adolescent locked attentively to the annual talk about sex in the youth group, explanations were so vague that one needed a map reference, a gift of interpretation and a copy of *Grays Anatomy* (the medical textbook, not the eternal television series), to figure out what was being shared.

I have occasionally struggled to be a truth-teller myself. An American Christian publisher recently told me that I was "too honest for the church". Spot the error, there, people...

Hence my delight that Tania has written this compelling, warm, practical, and utterly inspirational book. She begins by bluntly sharing some of her own fractures and fragilities, which is one reason I like her, and this book, a lot. No ivory towered exhortations here; rather another broken but under construction soul sharing some poignantly relevant advice with her fellow travellers.

Tania has a beautiful smile, which, helpfully, she uses a lot. But this is not the superficial grin of an enthusiastic airhead who wants to palm us off with platitudes, but is the facial architecture of one who has been around the proverbial block, has plenty of cuts and bruises to show for it, and now, in plain, unfussy language, wants to help the rest of us out. Here, you won't be bossed around, rudely shoved with a stack of *musts* and *shoulds*. But you will find a winsome invitation to live healthily, but not clinically.

So I won't say, "enjoy the book", because I *know* you will. OK, if you're of a nervous disposition, proceed with care. But I know that as a result of your walking through the pages that follow, you'll laugh, cry, be relieved, become resolved, and most important of all, be a more authentic follower of Jesus as you do.

Thanks, Tania.

Thanks a lot. Really.

Jeff Lucas

Introduction

Mine was a complex journey into adulthood.

Aged ten, I started puberty. By eleven, our family life was under pressure and cracks were beginning to show in my relationship with my parents. When I was twelve, I had the physical form of an eighteen-year-old. Aged thirteen I was sexually active, smoking, and drinking. By sixteen, I had left home and was working in pubs and sharing a single bed with my older boyfriend, a drayman with a brewery. By the time I was seventeen, I had been groomed by a local couple to become a stripper. (Thankfully, I never did execute my debut performance in a working men's club in the North East of England. The act before me was too good and I sharply left the venue!) I already had a few low budget glamour photo shoots under my belt by the time I was eighteen, and when I was nineteen a male "friend" was offering to pimp me out for £300 per session without a condom. It was an offer I declined. But that was a shocking and defining moment in which I realized how dark my life was becoming.

I was in a mess.

But the tides did turn: by the time I was twenty I was working as an administrator for a FTSE 100 company. I was still vulnerable, but was managing to hold down what now felt like a "career" and I was meeting a different breed of people. Articulate people. Ambitious people. People with aspiration.

And it rubbed off.

A year later and I was on a fast-track management training scheme; by twenty-five I was travelling the world as a global buyer, negotiating international contracts and managing supply chain logistics. A not dissimilar story to the 1988 film *Working Girl*, where a young Staten Island-raised working-class lass conquers all and ends up in the mergers and acquisitions department of a Wall Street investment bank.

It was an adventure indeed!

I could drink with the boys, play hard, yet still wake up early and nail a deal. As one colleague-turned-dear-friend said, "You're a sight to behold in the boardroom and even more so when dancing on it!" – referring to the penchant I had in those days to combine business with fun!

Oh my. I can laugh now.

Not long after that, I became a Christian. And with gusto, I listened to God and everything was turned on its head. I sold up and flew to Sydney, Australia, where I found an excellent church and Bible college. Here I spent nearly three years studying, learning, and listening to God. Since then I've been a church pastor; worked for urban-mission organizations; co-founded a community home caring for homeless teenagers; worked for large Christian charities; and now serve on a variety of boards whose concerns span the delivery of healthcare, education, and the abolition of child sexual exploitation. I'm also the group director for a wonderful organization that runs a chain of schools and well-being projects. But the *pièce de résistance*, the thing I'm most exhilarated by, has been adopting two courageous little boys. I not only feel vocationally fulfilled, but also maternally and spiritually fulfilled through my work and motherhood. Deeply satisfying.

Ah, you think, feeling mildly relieved for me. *Life's all sorted then!*

I cough, embarrassed.

I don't want to burst the "bubble of comfort" on this happy, grace-filled, life-turned-around story. But burst I must. Because since coming to faith fourteen years ago, the journey has been a paradox of passion and pain in equal measure. I haven't had the "Ta-da! Look, see – everything's OK now" experience, which so often accompanies my type of story in Christian magazine articles or platform testimonies.

That said, life deals us all a unique hand. We each have a different story and a different experience. And none of us, whether Christian or not, are exempt from both trials and joys. And trials I am all too familiar with. Matthew 5:45 sums this up: "He causes his sun to rise on the evil and the good, and sends rain on the righteous and the unrighteous."

I've learned that no amount of faith will stop bad things happening to good people. Nor good things happening to bad people! Nor good people making mistakes, and bad people making wise choices and vice versa!

While the mess-ups, which are actually of my own doing, aren't as frequent now as they were in my teens and twenties, I'm still well able to turn a situation from serenity into chaos surprisingly quickly. And disappointments, heartache, failures, and challenges have been regular visitors to the table. Not a popular, victorious, evangelical admission!

In fact, since coming to faith I've encountered multiple heart-breaking bereavements; made poor financial choices; lost confidence through redundancy; suffered a significant relationship breakdown; failed at ministry endeavours; struggled with people's unmet expectations in me and vice versa; had a near breakdown; have aspirations as yet not even close to seeing lived out; deeply grieved through two miscarriages; and all too regularly, clock up significant social faux pas. I am not the right girl to ask for a testimony at a prosperity conference plugging a "just believe it and it's yours, in the name of Jes-us-ah" agenda!

Nowadays my most common dilemma, amid a raging drama or two, is feeling frustrated that I haven't dealt with something as well as I might. Or at least being left with that feeling of "I'm sure there's something I could have done differently there."

Do you ever find yourself asking that? I intuitively know how I'd like something to turn out – I plan the gracious response to something or someone who's totally irked me, I make a personal pact to withhold a sharp word, or respond with grace… and sometimes I end up failing. And I'm left with a feeling of "not good enough" and disappointment in myself because I feel I should have either the skills, the insight, or the emotional intelligence to have oriented it well.

So, as you see, I stand before you metaphorically naked, with the intent of offering up my struggles, my mess-ups, and my less-refined moments. But hopefully not self-indulgently. Nor sensationally. Rather, for the purpose of learning – for the both of us. Now, in middle age, I'm finally learning to eyeball the "tough-stuff", mess-ups and "not done wells". I hear a cheer rising! I'm embracing the failures, fears, flops, and fiascos. I see them differently now. No longer do I see them as cringe-worthy black marks, nor as a personal immaturity that I'll eventually grow out of. And most importantly I don't now mark myself down as unredeemable nor beyond the love or grace of God. Quite the opposite.

I now see those failures, fears, flops, and fiascos as an opportunity. To be kind to myself, then to breathe… and then even more remarkably, to learn. American scholar Brené Brown, discussing kindness, asserts, "Talk to yourself like you would to someone you love."[1] I tried it. I'm changed because of it. The kindness that I now afford myself has liberated me to learn from difficult situations, rather than beat myself up because of them. And kindness toward myself has also allowed me the privilege of seeing quite how magnificent aspects of me really are. And as exciting, to see quite how magnificent aspects of others really are! It affects everything.

So I now live my life through what I like to call "kindsight", rather than mere hindsight. It's not just theory: it informs how I interpret and accept the past, negotiate and enjoy the present, and remain optimistic for the future.

Might I assume that you're in possession of this book because you need a little encouragement? Perhaps you need to know there's light at the end of the tunnel and that all might

1   "Brené Brown on the 3 Things You Can Do to Stop a Shame Spiral", as told to Oprah Winfrey, *Oprah's Lifeclass*, Oprah Winfrey Network (http://www.oprah.com/oprahs-lifeclass/Brene-Brown-on-the-3-Things-You-Can-Do-to-Stop-a-Shame-Spiral-Video).

turn out OK. Perhaps life hasn't dealt you a good hand but you're determined to see the positives nevertheless. Perhaps a mistake is costing you dearly and you feel sick to the stomach now dealing with the consequences. Perhaps you can't quite believe a situation can be redeemed, and you need some volts of faith to kick-start a new way of thinking. The principle of kindsight can aid this: it encourages us to live honestly and openly, not eradicating huge swathes of the past or present; nor daily reliving the scenario with zero constructive outcome – but embracing, accepting, and learning instead.

We might not be able to change what's happened, but we can change our continued response to it. And God wants to be in on every part of this journey, not just the parts of life we feel OK about, or are proud enough of. God wants to breathe goodness and kindness and love into every area of our life – particularly the areas we're the most frightened or ashamed of.

What you'll find on these pages are insights from my own story and those of others, gathered through the tough stuff of life: insights seen through kindsight. They're not always pretty, nor neatly packaged, but they're earthy and real.

The challenge I place before us is to dare to master kindsight. It's a game changer.

So, if life's been tough; it's not gone great; if you've messed up; if you don't feel as though you've dealt with something well – don't beat yourself up… instead, breathe, then ask: "What did I learn?" And apply a large slab of kindsight.

1

On Missing the Point of Church

You may have understandably made the assumption from the early part of the introduction that I grew up in a tumultuous family situation worthy of a *Jeremy Kyle* or *Jerry Springer* episode, given my then apparent predilection to general dysfunction and sexual exploration from a very young age. I've often noted how people who only know the headlines of my life try to analyse why my early years were so erratic. I've been asked countless times whether I was abused, which, while a sound diagnostic question, wasn't the case.

Another question, albeit asked only once was, "Were you copying your mother's behaviour? Was she promiscuous?", which, if you had known my lovely mum, is a hilarious notion, given her endearing prudish tendencies and penchant for woollen knee-length socks accompanied by Scholl clogs – not to mention her being faithful to a thirty-year marriage.

I may never know quite why things "ran off the rails" for me. It certainly wasn't due to a chaotic childhood or to abusive parents.

In fact, my childhood – certainly up to about eleven years old – was as good as one could hope for. Remarkably surprising given that I sported a severe 1960s bowl-haircut into the early eighties, wore harsh National Health glasses from age seven, and had a dicky hip that required crutches for six months! Not a winning combination, but I survived!

I recall blackberry-picking, narrow boat holidays, copious bike rides with my older sister, acrobatics in the back garden on an old mattress, and no real traumas at primary school, bar a boy called Alex pulling his trousers down and showing me his private parts. For someone looking from the outside in, we were a fairly typical British family. Mum, Dad, older sister, and me. My parents were from working-class stock, both with no small amount of challenging family history. Dad had secured himself an apprenticeship and worked very hard studying for an HND in mechanical engineering. This had led on to a fulfilling, but nonetheless stressful, career for him in design engineering. A non-fatal heart attack aged forty-five on the M40 motorway into work one day attested to this. Mum was a product of her time, a highly personable lady but with little career aspiration or self-confidence. She adored amateur dramatics, singing, and being a housewife, and she was very good indeed at these things. When my sister and I were very young my parents became Christians – the born-again, Spirit-filled, Bible-believing, evangelical variety. Church was central and Jesus was referred to as "Jesus my personal Lord and Saviour", in case there was any confusion as to who He was. And so, that's what I grew up in, was surrounded by, and assumed its identity by osmosis. Life as a child largely revolved around two things: Dad's work (plus the associated pressure, stress, absence, intrigue, income, and inevitable house moves around the country), and Christianity.

I was of a happy disposition as a child. Still am. Yet I also had the capacity to react quickly and respond emotionally rather than objectively. Still do. "Highly expressive" was often the diplomatic title afforded me by teachers and parents. Still is! It was dependent on how sincerely and respectfully someone engaged with me that determined whether my self-expression toward them was warm and effervescent or withdrawn and difficult. As a teenager, if you'd have brushed me against an egotistical authoritarian whose own voice was the only one they'd listen to, filled with dour opinion, unexplained instructions and legalistic assumption – oh man, I'd have to quickly get out of their way lest my mouth and attitude take over, often landing myself in hot water! I'd like to believe my responses now are a little more refined!

As I've been told by more than one source, I was not an easy to child to raise (lest you be concerned for my emotional well-being, I'm smiling, mischievously, as I'm writing). "Highly expressive" was also accompanied by "intense and intentional". If I felt it, I felt it 100 per cent. Add to that the early onset of puberty and large doses of raging hormones… well, things were not always pretty!

As you probably gather by now I wasn't fitting well into the "good Christian girl" box. And in the day when sayings such as "little girls should be seen and not heard", or "be a good little girl" were still mildly acceptable, I picked up the suggestion that I therefore wasn't "pleasing". I remember registering that quiet, obedient children were superior in some sense. And by default, I was inferior.

At twelve years of age, I can clearly remember an internal shift happening. Even though not a lot had changed externally. Chicken à la Rosemary (my mum, Rosemary's, name for a chicken casserole, exotic only by virtue of adding garlic!) was still being served every Monday night, gymnastics was still on Wednesdays, we were allowed a ten-penny bag of sweets on a Friday night after fish and chips, and *Juliet Bravo* was still my favourite TV programme. But, outside of this normality I was beginning to see some things differently and I was becoming unsettled with what I saw.

I began to see my parents' Christian faith for what felt like the first time. I guess this isn't altogether unusual: as children grow up they begin to question things they've always just accepted. But for me, sadly, faith shifted in my mind from being a normal "everyone does it" kinda thing, to an abnormal "I wish we didn't do it" kinda thing. Not only did I suddenly recognize that we actually went to church when others didn't, but I began to notice aspects that became oddities to me. I noticed behaviour at church, for example, that wasn't present at any other point in the week at home. Sunday's "Praise the Lord!" greeting, songs sung in a certain way, phrases used all seemed, in my naivety, to be altogether different from how we lived and expressed ourselves for the rest of the week. I wanted to see a Sunday face that was the same as the Monday to Saturday face. I'm sure this is also true for many Christian households across the country as well.

Then I noticed that certain ways of speaking and expressing things were different dependent on where we were. Religious language was used within church circles, but not at the shops or school. This didn't escape my attention.

The fracture lines of faith were forming for me.

I was facing a serious disconnect. The incredible Bible stories – so faithfully told to me – of burning bushes, parting of waves, men being swallowed whole by whales, lions being tamed in pits, local women becoming queens — certainly whetted my appetite and inspired me to want to trust in this God. But I had no obvious place to associate or connect these stories within my daily, average, really-quite-boring existence.

Hearing in youth groups about miracles, good overcoming evil in a swashbuckling kinda way and demons being cast out, and then reading about drug addicts being healed of their addictions in books by people like Jackie Pullinger and Nicky Cruz all seemed so exciting at the time. Yet, like many teenagers (and tweenagers), it just didn't relate to the rest of my life between the bookends of each of my monotonous-breakfast-school-homework-tea-sleep days. Dad still worked away during the week, Mum still baked wholemeal rock cakes, my sister still liked floral print, and I was still wearing glasses.

The radical revolutionary I had grown up learning about – Jesus – didn't seem quite so radical or revolutionary in everyday life, where scenes from the pages of the Good News Bible weren't played out. Certainly not in the town where I lived, anyway.

To add to my growing teenage faith-conundrums, over the years I'd seen "predicaments" in our church community unfolding in front of me that didn't always look good. I can clearly recall a church elder who left his young family for his vivacious secretary. A mum of four smoked so many cigarettes due to her nerves that her lips and fingers were yellow. A local reverend of a posh Anglican church was rumoured to not believe in Jesus. One of the choir would add a two-second warble on the end of every hymn or chorus stanza so that her voice would dominate, just like her opinions. Parents would protectively gather around their children when a certain single hairy member of the congregation came too close. The Christian music teacher was so very angry, all the time. Another church member wore sunglasses even on rainy days to cover bruises. One individual was diagnosed with "religious mania", where she stayed in a permanent state of manifesting encounters with the Holy Spirit, even when in the supermarket, walking around physically lurching and loudly groaning. And added to this, church was really, really boring.

In the eyes of a disenfranchised young person, all this stuff becomes odd and frightening – and if not frightening then mildly humorous. And if church isn't addressing or balancing these issues of life with great biblical teaching and a radical manifesto of what it is to live in God's Kingdom on earth, as in heaven – then what's left is not likely going to cut it for the average young person.

Like many teenagers, I developed a not altogether unsurprising reticence towards our family's involvement in church life. Maybe, like me, this happened to you? Or to your children? It can be an incredibly unsettling thing, for both children and parents. Some kids are perhaps scared that they'll lose the love of a parent for challenging the family status quo, or some will simply use it as a way to pull away from perceived parental control and assert their growing opinion. Some, as in my case, just didn't "get it". Parents then react, scared perhaps that their precious children may walk away from faith, and of course them, and what they represent. And the reaction, in turn, pushes the child further away. Painful stuff. It is such a common story. If you're relating to this, please know you're not alone.

My reticence was due to the fact that being a Christian didn't *seem* to make a jot of difference. In my childlike mind, it didn't actually make stuff OK, nor even come across as appealing. Also, and worryingly, somehow I'd picked up the message that to be a Christian meant that nothing should go wrong, God will protect you, and if He doesn't, either you're sinning or you're not saved. What terrible theology. I cringe by just typing it!

Recently Adrian Plass, the great faith-inspired comic genius, wrote a letter:

> *Sorry. [This is m]ore of a rant than a letter. Perhaps it's because these issues have become particularly important to me recently. In the course of this month I've lost most of the use of my right hand because of a stroke, together with something akin to neuralgia, also connected with the stroke, which causes a continual, throbbing headache. It's a long haul, and the future is uncertain, but medication and hard work are already beginning*

to show results. The thing I want to make clear, though, is however sh[**]ty things get, they will never be a measure of God's love for me or those who are close to me. Terrible things happen to Christians. They die in car crashes. They become paralysed. Businesses fail. Dreams plummet. Nightmares become reality. Our leader was crucified. If we can't beef up our puny little theology by embracing and incorporating these inescapable facts we might as well give up our ridiculous faith and join the Ember Day Bryanites. They do coffee and biscuits. They'll do.

Not for me. I'm in for the long haul, stroke or no stroke.

Yours, written with my left hand
Adrian.[2]

Very sad as I was about hearing he'd suffered a stroke, I loved reading this letter because it's real and so very honest about the tough stuff of life. Honest and yet still absolutely faith-filled. In my forties, I now know that God exists alongside the pain, and until a new heaven and new earth, it would seem, bad things aren't going to be eradicated. But Jesus is here with us, every step of the way. In the midst of the suffering. Now that's better theology.

Back in my childhood I needed something that was so much more real. I needed to know about a God who is there

2   Published on his website, June 2014 (http://www.adrianplass.com/june2014.htm).

through all the realities of life: the ups, downs, adventures, and humdrum bits. And I needed to know how to deal with the downright difficult bits.

What was absent for me as a child growing up in the church was an honesty to help me understand what was happening. As an adult, and with kindsight, I now understand that faith itself isn't complicated, but the way humanity represents it and lives it makes it complicated! Because we are complicated. Life is complicated. We live in a fallen, less-than-perfect world, so it follows that church isn't going to escape the complication – because we *are* the church!

My friend Andy Frost eloquently captured the great teenage disconnect I felt when he emailed me years ago, saying, "We teach good, sound, Christian values like respect, integrity and good moral conduct. But we have often forgotten to teach our kids other great Christian values like risk, generosity and courage. We have presented a nice Jesus rather than a radical Jesus." This fully resonated with me. As a teenager, I wanted something to sink my teeth into and have an adventure with – what young person doesn't?

When faith becomes about a Sunday outing, niceties, rules, regulations, moral codes, pretence, and an "in-language", the integrity of the whole thing implodes for many young people, as it did for me. Of course, the challenge is that we adults have to live the fully courageous, HD, surround-sound version of faith in order to showcase it. To our youngsters! Because we have to ask ourselves, what are they seeing in us? Boredom, apathy, back-biting? Or fresh ways of doing things, embracing edgy mission accompanied by prayerful sacrifice? However imperfectly!

Some kids survive church. Others don't just survive, they thrive – given a loving, supportive church, a great group of friends in the youth group, and youth leaders who inspire them. It's all about their individual experience in the wider picture. But for others, even under the best circumstances, church and the notion of God just don't cut it. My sister, for example, flourished. Whereas, in the exactly the same conditions as her, I just didn't survive. Same family, two sisters, two different reactions.

If you're a parent reading this, and one of your children hasn't survived church or has turned away from faith, please don't blame yourself. Please don't read Proverbs 22:6, contending that Scripture validates the claim that if we had taught our sons and daughters the right values, they would not have departed from the faith – and crumble at the accusation. Please don't! Kindsight is needed in huge measure here. Many factors, many people, many Christians, over many years, will have impacted your child. Not just you. Your child also has a right to make personal choices that cannot be dictated by even the most well-intentioned parent. If your teens aren't the toe-the-line type, whatever you do or say may not work to keep them at church. In fact, the opposite might work better. The very act of gently respecting their choice, however hard, instead modelling a supportive Christian life (possibly with some risk and adventure mixed in!), trusting God and praying like the clappers – and you never know, their faith may be ignited in later life. As it did with me.

Thankfully, since my teenage years, an excellent book has been written, which I highly recommend for anyone reading this chapter and needing support. It's Rob Parsons' terrific *Getting Your Kids through Church without them Ending up Hating God*.[3] Every Christian family needs a copy. Every *church* needs a copy. I wish I'd written it – it was begging to be penned!

So, in my youth, spiritual confusion, poor theology, and church experiences that were unappetizing took their toll. What also entered into the arena was a crippling lack of identity. In certain churchy circles I pretended I belonged to Jesus, to the church, and its sub-culture. And yet, in school and elsewhere, I was another person, seemingly happier, but with different values, beliefs, and opinions. There is no explanation for this other than I wanted to please my parents and to "belong", yet I also wanted to "belong" in the non-church space – at school, at clubs, with friends and their families – so I acted in a completely different way. Deep fragmentation began to happen.

By my early teens, I was leading two different emotional lives. This was very destructive because it hampered my ability to manage the child-to-youth and youth-to-adult transition. And when a young person has little sense of identity, all manner of behaviours can exhibit themselves. Quite literally, I didn't know who I was, what my values were, what to trust, or how to feel or safely process emotions.

The list of struggles was growing. There were more and more family arguments. I had a deepening anxiety that there was something fundamentally wrong with me and my attitude

3   Monarch Books, 2011.

was worsening. School was at least fun due to the friendships I had, and it was a welcome respite from home. Smoking had become an addiction, not just a school bus hobby. The "little girls should be seen and not heard" ditty internally mocked me; shame abounded, condemnation was rife. I suffered guilt and shame at giving my new boyfriend oral sex all too readily; infatuation and lust became the norm; I started drinking alcohol. In summary: for me it was a tough, tough gig being a teenager with a foot in the church and a foot and an arm outside of it.

Now of course I'm not saying this is the experience of all teenagers who feel a disconnection between church and other aspects of their lives. But they may share some of the confusion and disillusion, and they may have a journey experimenting with who they are and what they believe. Thankfully, for most, that doesn't mean they will necessarily strike out in the same ways as I did.

But in my extreme confusion, I was becoming more and more unable to reconcile faith with life and life with faith. I was confused by what I saw, confused by what I was doing, confused by how faith didn't seem to make an impact, and confused about everyone's seeming avoidance of talking about difficult issues that were right in front of them. I was coming to all sorts of poor theological and personal assumptions that, sadly, had no safe space to be tested and re-engineered. Not at home, nor at church, and not at youth group nor in school.

A simple, if not painful reality, was that there were too few adults modelling a fun-filled, aspirational, inspirational, healthy

Christian identity yet who were honest about life and all its challenges and who were prepared to have a continual, messy, truthful interchange with me about how faith and life worked. Which for an expressive, extrovert live wire such as myself, was vital. And it was vitally missing.

In the spirit of kindsight, I've learned that for Christians to live a life where faith is out-worked transparently and openly with no hidden corners, acknowledging life's challenges and disappointments, as well as its joys, is priceless. If we pretend suffering doesn't exist or, indeed, if we live permanently in suffering, how can we model a life that is seen as trusting a real and living God? I want to be real and model the truth that, if we let Him, He will live with us through every moment of joy as well as any suffering as we travel through our difficulties until more settled times are reached.

Similarly, when we Christians fail and occasionally blow it, as undoubtedly we will, it's best not to cover it up. Own it. Walk people through our struggle in an appropriate way. We can learn from it ourselves and, by being transparent, we can allow others to learn too. That's how to showcase to other people an authentic faith that can survive failure in life and still yet rise to take on another day. Young people particularly need to see this. Young people can spot a cover-up from a million miles away and their interpretation is "fake". They'd much rather know the truth of a difficult situation and how you've negotiated it in a Christian way, than for adults to gloss over tricky situations. Being real is also all about admitting that the truth is you don't know all the answers. Sometimes, we need to model patience while waiting for God to reveal His plan in the journey of our lives. It's much better to help others orient their faith by never shying away from any subject, however uncomfortable we may find it.

"Do as I say, not do as I do" is a death-knell statement to young people. Instead of bending their ears with dogma, give them room to work out their theology, however much it clashes with our own. Listen and learn together. This is the Kingdom way.

Actions speak louder than words… what do young people see when they look at their parents? Faith or self-reliance? Forgiveness or anger? Anger-induced discipline or benevolence? Generosity or selfishness? Are parents living the radical lives they desire their children to be living? To live a Christ-centred contagious life and to model a whole-life faith is how the next generation will be inspired. Our teenagers need to see us living with purpose and with passion for a great cause. In other words, being people who embody a radical, risky, and real relationship with Jesus.

For me, it took fifteen further years for God to begin to sort out the "faith-mess" I'd got into, and another fourteen years on from that I'm still working on it!

I have learned so much from my experiences. I don't beat myself up any more, I just put the learning into practice. I make it matter. It's why I hugely enjoy working with young Christians, mentoring and guiding them into a whole-life experience of their faith.

Imagine if we all helped just one young person and stuck by them, no matter what; if we were utterly unconditional in our commitment to them. Being there for them, taking them out for a hot chocolate, allowing them to ask any questions, talk about any subject, confess any silly goings-on (or indeed serious goings-on!) without making them feel as though they've blown it for life, nor condemning them, but instead actively coaching them through different choices for next time a tricky scenario is thrown up.

I wonder if we would have a church still full of our young, who feel confident to experiment with life still, knowing we're there to provide a safety net for them. And ultimately with them knowing how much they are loved by a huge and passionate God who would love nothing more than for them to step into their calling and potential now. I don't want them to miss the point about church like I did. Church can be, and is, a glorious thing.

2

On Families that Implode

Family life continued for me on the same trajectory – downwards – with cracks appearing and increasing to canyon-like size, caused by the challenging chemistry between my family and me. By the time I was fifteen, power struggles were occurring with tiring regularity.

Mum and I would fight. A lot. Every fight mattered, but very few were meaningful. We'd go into the ring of emotional wrestling, round after round "ding, ding" on the most ridiculous of issues, such as whether I was wearing too much mascara to school that morning or whether I had walked the dog far enough if at all (a handsome young man lived just round the corner and the dog would end up tied to a tree close by, sorry me ol' canine friend, now long gone). And if there were no clear winner of the fight, Dad would be brought in – upon coming home from work, tired and drained. On some occasions he'd become adjudicator, on others, he'd just try and exit. I recall him once saying, "I'm stuck between a rock and a hard place, love – she's my wife and you're my daughter". Retrospectively, I feel pained he was placed in the middle; he wasn't then, or now, a man who was wired to manage conflict. Then we'd all have a few days off to recover, each stepping gently around the other, until the next trigger was set off. Then the emotional battle would start all over again. Occasional pledges of surrender were made by each of us and varying peace tactics were employed. But nothing much worked. We were all becoming war-weary.

With kindsight I can see that the things we fought over, weren't actually the things we thought we were fighting over. That's not meant to be a riddle! If the issue on the surface was, let's say, the wearing of too much mascara, the real issue beneath was that my mum felt embarrassed by how I looked going to school. Her dream was for her daughters to do well, to succeed. She thought this was more likely to be achieved through me being a "good girl", behaving in a certain way. This also involved Mum wanting me to wear knee-length skirts and model-like natural skin, rather than presenting as something from St Trinian's – a look that I sported particularly well! With a spirit of kindness and understanding I can now see that it was devastating for my parents that I appeared to be rejecting so much of what they wanted from and for me, not least, as we discussed in the previous chapter, their faith.

And so it was with the majority of our arguments: they were a front for painful issues going on underneath, whether it was them feeling powerless, me feeling suppressed, them wanting respect, or me wanting to be accepted as I was, rather than what I perceived as them wanting a "different" me, or for me to live up to the high standards my older sister was, albeit subconsciously, setting. That's not to knock her of course – she just so happened to be making wiser decisions than I was – but that didn't stop it hurting, that I couldn't please my parents, even when I did try, because I just couldn't compete with my older sister who had the opposite temperament to me. And so the gulf between sisters also grew.

This general confusion is not unusual within families. Often, the things we argue about are not really what the argument's about. It's worth the effort of digging down beneath the surface of an argument, as you may well uncover a nugget of emotional gold that is of great value to your family. If you can identify the root cause of the arguments, it will be much easier to address the real issue and halt further conflict, in turn then bringing things to a place where conversation can happen.

Enlightenment comes therefore once we understand what we're actually arguing about. Perhaps we should all take stock of our last argument and ponder: "Was that really about the subject of the argument? Or was it a subconscious front for some underlying issue that needs addressing?" I can't tell you how many arguments I have managed to avoid by recognizing early on that I needed a conversation about something specific rather than an argument about something trivial!

We should also acknowledge with kindsight that everyone within a family brings with them their own interpretation, understanding, and experience. And as a result, we may never fully understand the complexity of the family dynamics in play. There is often generational baggage to contend with (roles people play, or cemented behaviours: "Well, that's how my mother did it", and the like) and also private and personal baggage – that all collides in the space of "family". It may never be fully understood, analysed, or unpacked, but it will be there.

This is the case for biological families, and even more so for those with adopted members or blended families.

However we may interpret something, we can't deny family members their own perspectives. Many of us do this by refusing to acknowledge others' experiences or not accepting their understanding of how something has developed. This is in large part because we all just want to be "right". Sentences we hurl at each other such as "You've got that all wrong, it's like this" or "No, no, no, just listen, a better way of viewing it is...". Superiority, dictating, and enforcing a way of thought on to someone changes very little. Neither does speaking over someone, not allowing someone to finish a sentence, using control tactics, or belittling someone – this is bullying. Instead, openness, trying to really understand the other's perspective even *if* we disagree, and embracing the option *to* disagree are a really constructive ways forward. These also allow for the jewel of learning to be held, rather than holding the stone of "being right".

What is readily available to every member of a family who is encountering difficulties is for everyone to take responsibility. At least in part, for what they have contributed to the situation. It takes more than one person to contribute to a dysfunctional relationship. There may be obvious let-downs that need to be acknowledged by an offending individual, but invariably, there will also be influencing factors both consciously and/or subconsciously added by the one who perceives themselves as the non-offending party, which all culminate in something broader going wrong. By developing and evolving this mind-set of taking responsibility, it helps to mitigate against victim–perpetrator mentality, which rarely solves anything. We are all victims when a family implodes. And when candidly reviewed, we are all also perpetrators, even if it's by the smallest sliver of the pie.

And with this balanced approach, it would be kind of us to accept that there's nothing inherently "wrong with them" or "wrong with us" if family life actually breaks down. After all, we are all fallen from grace.

Now, our actions may have been wrong. Theirs may have been wrong. Our attitudes may have been wrong. Their attitudes may have been wrong. Each of our expectations may have been wrong. But what's not wrong is the essence of who we each are, our unique self. We are loved passionately by God. And all are worthy of good and wholesome relationships. Fully worthy. Each and every one of us, regardless of our history.

No one chooses a family breakdown. We may not have played our best game, nor done all we should, nor loved well – and we each need to accept that. And with honesty, reflection, and repentance face facts. What we can't allow is a pervading sense of shame to ride roughshod through our whole being that says "there must be something wrong with me". This cannot take up residence in our souls (see the chapter on shame).

One of my deepest personal lessons applying kindsight to my own life is that past performance (either by me, or others) or experience within family (however dysfunctional) don't dictate our future. Let me say that again. For my own benefit.

Past performance, negative experiences, let-downs, broken relationships within family – whether mother to daughter, father to son, husband to wife, sibling to sibling – do not dictate the quality of our future relationships. Only present and future choices can do that.

And if we submit to God, the most gracious, committed Father we could ever hope to have – and are leaning in on Him to help with our present choices coupled with *learning* from the past, and not beating ourselves up – then there's every reason to imagine we can relationally construct something significant, joyous, elegant, and sustainable in the future.

Readers and friends, I get emotional talking about it. Because we so rarely grab this truth. The truth is that we are a loved, forgiven people. We are forgiven. Others are forgiven. We can each, every one of us, start again when it's not gone well. The expectations placed on us from others and expectation of ourselves can be released, if we would only let them go. And we can be free to recognize our frailty. And embrace that we are never going to get it right all the time. Sometimes we will succeed, and we should celebrate our successes. But other times we will fail. We are not super-powered, turbo-charged perfect beings; we are weak, and made from dust. Yet born in the image of the Almighty and loved beyond measure.

This is a powerful concept if we would just absorb it and let our souls digest it into every part of who we are. Scripture speaks this out loudly when it says in the psalms:

For his unfailing love toward those who fear him
is as great as the height of the heavens above the earth.
He has removed our sins as far from us
as the east is from the west.
The Lord is like a father to his children,
tender and compassionate to those who fear him.
For he knows how weak we are;
he remembers we are only dust.

Psalm 103:11–14

So let's embrace His tenderness and compassion for us. Never doubting it, even when it's tempting to think that we're "too much" for this heavenly grace. Some of us have the propensity to conclude that everyone else is worthy of this grace, just not us. Codswallop. It is a lie we allow ourselves to be told. His love is "as great as the height of the heavens above the earth" (Psalm 103:11).

By grabbing on to this grace and love from God, I have managed to interpret my relationship with my mum constructively, so that I can learn from it and stop beating myself up about it. I now understand that Mum saw obedience from me as a form of love, and disobedience as rejection. Not a good formula for either her or me, especially with our temperaments. I was always going to have a propensity to be disobedient as part of testing boundaries, and Mum was always going to feel that as rejection, because of her childhood family experiences. Sadly, her father left when she was but a little girl, leaving the remaining family in a vulnerable position. Also, I suspect, upon reflection, words of affirmation and physical touch were the ways she was most comfortable with when it came to expressing and receiving affection. Neither of these came naturally from a hurting, stroppy teenager!

Kindsight and learning from my relationship with my mum have shown me that parenting is a hard gig. It's a job with no description, a daily challenge with marginal support, and an emotional roller coaster with no seat belt.

Granted nowadays there is a lot more help out there, not least some excellent parenting books, which just weren't available when my parents were on the crazy child-raising journey. Any good library or bookshop has shelves groaning under the weight of titles along the lines of "Top ten tips for successful parenting"! My family needed a book back then that helped explain how to direct all my teenage energy (aka strong-willed and chaotic!) in a constructive way. I feel no bitterness, just a sadness that more help wasn't available to us, a family. We had so much unrealized potential, that, instead of blossoming, imploded.

And the result was deep, deep frustration for all concerned in my family. The more compliant I was expected to be, the less I knew how to achieve it, and so the route of least resistance for my personality was to keep pushing outward, doing more of the very things that were causing the problems, because I was at least successful at these!

And so it was, that with parents unable to reach or relate to a highly expressive me, our family bounced along from one disagreement to another followed by meltdown to yet more polarized positions within the family.

Eventually I left home, just a few months after my sixteenth birthday. My mum had left a small clipping from a local newspaper on my bedside table that facilitated my departure. "Room to rent in 3-bedroomed house", it said. "£35.00 pw, bills included". My mum's actions here must be balanced by the fact that it was long preceded by my threatening to leave home – probably as regularly as once a week! Looking back, Mum must have reached the point of feeling that there was no other option. I needed no further encouragement. However, I still felt a jarring hurt over the non-verbalized "ejection", which I hid under a thick layer of eighties make-up.

The next day, instead of planning a move to rented accommodation, I moved every item from my bedroom into black plastic bin liners to the house of the highly disapproved of, gregarious, tousled, muscled older boyfriend. The expected pathways of my youth-to-adult life were gone in a blink of an eye. Family walks after Sunday lunch, gone. Choosing A-levels together, gone. Leaving for university, gone.

And for some years to come, until faith remoulded these experiences, I experienced life in the dark lane, detached yet compulsively attached to the wrong people; alone yet always popular; bright and engaging but internally doubtful and anxious; lacking in purpose and scared, yet outwardly driven and confident. The implosion of the family was very costly.

Family implosion is not unusual. Personality clashes, misunderstandings, out-and-out rejection, undiagnosed or medically unmanaged mental health issues, addictions – these are more common than we would ever wish to imagine. They deeply impact family life.

Serious issues such as undiagnosed or medically unmanaged mental health challenges and life-controlling addictions are particularly hard for families to orient because factors out of our control come into play. These include changes in personality, erratic behaviour, deception and possibly even violence. And even if, in the case of addiction, for example, an individual in the family is able to bring things under control, the feelings of fear and betrayal that family members are left with can still be very hard to get over and move on from.

However, if the issue, as was ours, is more about personalities and mis-matched aspirations, there's a lot that can be done at least to aid functional relationships. A spot of grace, wisdom to listen, even when your back's up, and keeping perspective all go a long way to creating healthy family dynamics. Might we take a minute now to reflect on how we might help a presently negative family relationship? Dare we offer out grace to someone when we feel that they least deserve it? Could we just listen to their side and not feel we have to justify ours? Would it be possible, with lashings of prayer, to keep perspective even though we might be boiling inside about something someone else has done?

Thinking with kindsight has helped me enormously in these areas. I now see that the job my parents had, to harness my big personality and extrovert expression, into a positive and well-directed space, was beyond their capability with the personal resources they had at the time. My parents loved me. I know they loved me. They just couldn't help me to be the best version of me. And neither could I help them be the best version of themselves: the version that was real, seen, and appreciated by many others but that I couldn't see.

A profound wave of grace from my heart swept over my parents a long time ago. And I believe the same happened from them toward me too. Years on, I've had even greater insights into their parenting world, particularly since working with young people, and of course, becoming a mother myself. I now know what it means to have your buttons pushed. And I now know how unpleasant it is when something becomes too much and the parent/child dynamic topples into child/child, where before long, both parties react.

At times, it feels like the effort and know-how required to simply de-escalate a potential meltdown requires the skill of a hostage negotiator. But therein is the key: parenting, particularly, is a skill that needs to be actively *learned*. It is rarely inherent. We need to be intentional and work hard at it: read up, listen to others, seek guidance, try out strategies, and apply buckets of patience. Isn't this the case too for every relationship in life?

The major challenge of parenting, as very parent knows, is that the goalposts keep changing. Just as you get used to a certain age and stage in a child's life, that child seamlessly moves on to the next stage so you, as the adult, need to do a bit of fancy footwork in seamlessly adjusting how you go about parenting this new stage. As if that's not difficult enough to negotiate, you can't necessarily rely on "knowing it all" if and when the next child comes along. A one-size-fits-all parenting style simply doesn't work, even within the same family. Perhaps this was why my parents found it a challenge to parent me, following as I did like a hurricane, after the relative calm of my more steady and persuadable sister. (That said, they did make attempts to help us both channel our different personalities and explore our individual interests, for instance encouraging us to attend different high schools – a more creative one for me, and the other more academic for my sister.)

The support of other friends and families, including of course our church community, can be a real help, especially when genuine life-sharing occurs rather than "Sunday morning turning-up". A healthy community is where parents, carers, and children can meaningfully share and really help each other by way of sharing experiences and in terms of practical support. We need other adults who love both the children and the parents, whose judgment values we respect, who can support us through all the difficult times and celebrate through the good. And we must not at all costs compare ourselves to other families. This gets us nowhere but paranoid, unsettled, and dismayed.

I would be lost without my church and community of Christian and non-Christian friends. One of my biggest sources of children's recipes, behavioural strategies, and general empathy comes from my dear mate and former PA, Katie, a mother of twins, who makes me scream with laughter at her take on things. Close friends Katy, Stella, and Jenny, between them mothers of seven children, have been constant teachers and prayerful support. Wonderful girlfriends such as Victoria and Katka are like the best of aunties, always on the look out for resources and ideas for Mack and Charlie, revelling in time too with the boys bonding. Best friends Heidi and Ed treat my boys as their own, faithfully encouraging me to "keep on keeping on", even when tired, bedraggled, and doubting my ability to mother.

It is, after all, a journey that none of us get right all of the time. It's a challenge. It can be messy. And, let's be real, some children are harder to handle than others. In the past, there might have been a tendency to remain very closed about this, particularly in church circles, for fear of incurring judgment from the Christian community. This may have been how my parents felt, for example, when it came to how much mascara I wore to school. Church communities and of course general friendship groups should be places where you can share how to deal with issues, praying and travelling through the journey of parenting together. To work, it requires complete confidentiality and a non-judgmental approach. In a loving environment, it is surprising, when you share the worries that have been keeping you awake at night, how often there is someone in the group who can apply a little kindsight for you. They might be further down the parenting line: they have been there, done that, and had similar challenges. They could bring comfort in a real, rather than theoretical way, and come alongside you as you prayerfully seek to apply a Herculean will to stay calm and an unswerving determination to see good in the child.

One particularly tough negotiation that has entered our modern world is the role of being a step-parent. My huge respect goes out to you if you are parenting in a blended family. Stepfamilies are, of course, the new "normal" as nearly half (42 per cent) of all marriages end in divorce in the UK[4] and the statistics for break-ups are higher for cohabiting couples.[5] So it is very likely that people will then move on into other new relationships, taking their children with them.

Of course, it's not just the involved parents who have negotiations to undertake, but also the children. By the parent entering into a new relationship, an "ex" is now replaced with a "new". The kids may or may not have love-relationships to maintain with their primary mum and dad, who are now the "ex". Then they're introduced to Mum's new partner or Dad's new partner (sometimes both) so already they have up to four "parental" relationships to orientate. Then they have biological siblings, step-siblings, and a whole load of new aunties, uncles, grandparents, and cousins. And if children are adopted, there's all of the above to negotiate plus another layer of genetic family to manage at some point.

The skills required to blend two families successfully cannot be underestimated and I applaud my many friends who

4   Office for National Statistics, "What percentage of marriages end in divorce?", 9 February 2013 (http://www.ons.gov.uk/ons/rel/vsob1/divorces-in-england-and-wales/2011/sty-what-percentage-of-marriages-end-in-divorce.html).
5   As reported in the Institute for Fiscal Studies 2010 briefing by Alissa Goodman and Ellen Greaves, "Cohabitation, marriage and relationship stability", p. 1. (http://www.ifs.org.uk/bns/bn107.pdf).

are orienting through this, at times, challenging maze. This is further put in perspective when we read Ron Deal from Focus on the Family's words:

> *Everyone wants "this marriage" to be their last… and to be healthy and strong. But many couples in blended families (also called stepfamilies) know that the odds are against them… While the U.S. divorce rate sits around 45 percent, the blended marriage divorce rate is approximately 67 percent (73 percent for third marriages).*

He continues,

> *I'm convinced many blended marriages fall prey to divorce because they get blindsided by the pressures and unforeseen dynamics of stepfamily living. Dating couples, for example, naively assume that their first-marriage taught them everything they need to know to have a happy re-marriage, and parents who raised their own children assume they know how to be a step parent. Generally speaking neither is the case.[6]*

There are families who are really struggling with this stuff and carrying guilt and pain, all of which escalate with each "failed" marriage. Particularly within the church, they may keep their

6 Ron Deal, "Remarriage and Blended Families", 2008 (http://www.focusonthefamily.com/marriage/marriage-challenges/remarriage-and-blended-families/the-smart-blended-marriage#ref1).

challenges hidden because they feel shame and embarrassment that not just one, but now two – or even more – relationships are proving too much. I know two God-loving stepfamilies who are on the verge of breakdown as I type. In the words of one husband, "We feel less able to ask for help, as we already feel as though we carry the stigma that we're second class Christians for having failed marriages behind us. To admit we're failing on this one feels so humiliating."

We need a second glance at this! It's not our job to judge their past, or question their relationship history. Our job, as a loving, serving community of people, is simply to be there, offering huge kindness first and foremost. It is remarkable what gets transmitted through our own lives out to others. Let's dig in with people. Deeply. Love them. Laugh with them. Lighten the load. Verbally and non-verbally showcase goodness and respect. If we do this, they are more likely to see success blossom within their family relationships as they draw upon the support so needed, and we ourselves will be blessed because we will more likely be shown the same love, care, and respect when we find ourselves in need of it. Yes, what goes around does come around. I have seen it too many times to believe anything different. I have always been pulled back to the Scripture of Matthew 7:1–5:

> Do not judge others, and you will not be judged. For you
> will be treated as you treat others. The standard you use
> in judging is the standard by which you will be judged.
> And why worry about a speck in your friend's eye when
> you have a log in your own? How can you think of saying

to your friend, "Let me help you get rid of that speck in your eye," when you can't see past the log in your own eye? Hypocrite! First get rid of the log in your own eye; then you will see well enough to deal with the speck in your friend's eye.

Boom. We couldn't get a clearer message, could we?

And this Scripture needs to be one that informs our spirits time and time and time again in regard to handling difficult family situations, our own or others', of whatever nature – be it child, parent, or sibling challenges, marital breakdown, betrayal, hurt, or general dislike! If we treat others as we wish to be treated, then we can sleep at night in the sure and safe knowledge that we are dealing with our own log, because we all have one. And that will ensure we can see just well enough to serve the needs of others even if it's not returned. It's just the Kingdom way.

3

On Shame and All Its Secrets

Humiliated. Ridiculed. Embarrassed. Unworthy. Incompetent. Have you ever felt like this? These feelings have a root cause of another, more powerful, and often painful, feeling – that of shame, the result of which is to leave the "sufferer" often feeling woefully inadequate. For some, it can be debilitating – paralysing even. Let's explore how this extreme emotion can play out in our everyday lives.

Shame, the silent destroyer

Shame has been significant in my life. A pervading sense of shame is probably one of the most destructive residues of my earlier years. Back then, shame crept into the tiny cracks, and filled out like expanding foam filler. Forces conspired together to use every negative event; every critical word spoken to me; every moment with family members that left me feeling misunderstood and alone; every disappointed look thrown in my direction when just being "me"; and of course every negative choice I made and the extensive raft of daft things I did – all ensured the whole was much bigger than the sum of the parts.

Shame was further induced by not *feeling* unconditionally loved, even though the reality was I was wanted, loved, and cared for. To not *feel* loved, whether it's true or perceived, allows the belief that "I'm unlovable" to take hold. Given we are wired both to be loved and to love, this is a deeply destructive belief. And to feel unlovable undermines positive self-esteem. Destructive one-liners can drop into our heads at any time, such as "If people *really* knew me, they'd walk away"; "I'm not as good as others"; or "I'm not acceptable as I am". When these one-liners occur regularly enough in our thoughts, and we accept them instead of challenging them, they become our version of truth and, as a result, our self-esteem is affected. These thoughts don't affect just our attitudes, but our behaviours too, as there is a direct correlation between the two. Our thoughts affect our feelings, our feelings affect our attitudes and our attitudes affect our behaviour. Unsurprising, then, that people with low self-esteem have an increase in negative, addictive, or self-punishing behaviours. The painful reality is that these negative behaviours only promote yet more shame and in turn heighten thought patterns that simply reaffirm to ourselves the very fact that we are unlovable. Oh what a vicious cycle! Friends, shame is a silent destroyer.

Resident shame

One of the outworkings of "resident shame" (my term for when shame is "at home" with us) is that the psyche allows the thought "there must be something wrong with me" to be processed whenever anything goes awry. Even if it's something we may have had no jurisdiction over. A long time ago, my car broke down, with the exhaust literally falling off the bottom of the car. I can clearly remember having a thought along the lines that it had happened because of being naughty when I was a child. What! A crazy shame-connection in my inner world had quickly fired into my brain resulting in that irrational thought. Things going wrong is an inevitable part of being human, and to consider that it's in essence who we are, or something we've historically experienced, or that there's something innately wrong with us that has caused the situation – is disastrous.

"I am something wrong" is an unhealthy psyche; "I may have done something wrong" is much healthier. Shame that has made its home in us, this "resident shame", will always encourage the unhealthy psyche to consider "I am something wrong". It's pivotal as men and women of faith that we work hard on shifting our internal belief to the healthy place of accepting what we may have contributed to "I may have done something wrong" instead of being sunk by the lie that "I am something wrong".

Difference between shame and guilt

To work hard on managing our internal beliefs requires self-awareness. And to be able to name shame, as self-awareness grows, is a remarkable step in itself. Once named, the step beyond this is to be able to differentiate between shame and guilt.

I only wish I had understood the difference in my teenage years, my twenties and my thirties! One of my heroines of the modern-day psychology scene is an awesome thinker and communicator called Brené Brown. She considers that guilt is not bad for us – in fact she states that she is "pro-guilt".[7] Guilt is good in that it keeps us on track, making sure that our behaviour aligns with our personal values. This is because we fear the discomfort that may arise when our behaviour doesn't match up to those values.

Her thinking is in a similar vein to the assertions I make in pointing at the outworkings of "resident shame". When a mistake is made, and someone is hurt, can we say, "I'm sorry, I made a mistake"? Healthy guilt would promote this. Shame, on the other hand, says "I'm sorry", but accompanied by the feeling that we *are* the mistake.

Guilt can promote positive change whereas shame just draws us further into its epicentre.

There are some varying degrees of thought around the very terminology and functionality of the word "shame", which is worth a balanced look. Luke Gilkerson, general editor and primary author of the *Covenant Eyes* blog (a blog to help individuals address sexual temptations and addictions), writes:

> *There can also be both true and toxic shame. If I have sinned against God and offended Him, or if I have sinned against another and hurt my relationship with them, I should feel a sense of shame. Shame is a healthy heart-response to the fact of a torn relationship.*[8]

7   For more on this see Brené Brown's article: "4 (Totally Surprising) Life Lessons We All Need to Learn", 14 June 2012 (http://www.oprah.com/spirit/Life-Lessons-We-All-Need-to-Learn-Brene-Brown/2).
8   Luke Gilkerson, "Guilt vs. Shame: Why Definitions Matter", 1

I understand entirely what Gilkerson is getting at here. True shame could also be a beneficial response to sin. Yet, experience would suggest that the line trodden on is a very narrow one as, whether true or toxic, shame has a habit of enlarging without permission. So, for the sake of keeping things simple (always my preferred route!), I'm with Brené on this, and would make the same distinction between guilt and shame as Gilkerson makes about true shame (what we are describing in this book as guilt) and toxic shame (as it says on the tin, stopped-you-in-your-tracks shame).

Earlier I shared an example of when I associated a car breaking down as being emotionally connected to being naughty as a child. I've not been alone in experiencing this type of shame-induced thought. I speak to many people who share with me that they struggle with this sense of "I'm sorry. I *am* a mistake" or "I am something wrong" shame. I have a chum in his forties: a gorgeous, intelligent, good-looking man, excellent career, widely respected in his profession and for his faith, with a happy and content family, committed church life, and a Yorkshire terrier – and yet due to feeling unloved in his childhood and somewhat belittled and sidelined, feels at times that he is "something wrong". He can be on a great run of things, and all it takes is one incident that in normal circumstances wouldn't outshine the rest of the good stuff, to cause him to shrivel, internalize, and convince himself that he's not good enough, period. It typically takes his determined, intuitive wife

February 2013 (http://www.covenanteyes.com/2013/02/01/guilt-vs-shame-why-definitions-matter/).

and the power of the Holy Spirit to help hydrate him again with truth, both emotional and spiritual; to restore him back into the fullness of himself. Does anyone relate to this?

I find more so now for me, that it's when a crisis hits, or I find myself in above my head, or when I feel unloved or rejected – that that's when feelings of shame try to take their opportunity to rise. I'm wiser to it now, however, and I'm pleased to report, and therefore celebrate, a growing and deepening resilience to it.

Thorn in the flesh

I sometimes wonder whether this propensity to "resident shame" isn't *my* "thorn in the flesh" that the apostle Paul shares he contended with, which to us, the reader, is still a mystery as to what his particular affliction was. In regard to my situation, perhaps I'm over-spiritualizing it, and over-analysing it, or both! Regardless, let's read it together: it's a cracking piece of Scripture.

In 2 Corinthians 12:7–10:

So to keep me from becoming proud, I was given a thorn in my flesh, a messenger from Satan to torment me and keep me from becoming proud. Three different times I begged the Lord to take it away. Each time he said, "My grace is all you need. My power works best in weakness." So now I am glad to boast about my weaknesses, so that the power of Christ can work through me. That's why I take pleasure in my weaknesses, and in the insults, hardships, persecutions, and troubles that I suffer for Christ. For when I am weak, then I am strong.

Likewise, my vulnerability in this area certainly does prevent me from falling into the trap of being "proud" – or "conceited" as the NIV puts it! And I take huge comfort in that the fact that the counter-cultural way of the Kingdom means that when I'm weak, I'm operating the most with trust and reliance in Jesus, and therefore I am profoundly strong. In Him. What a beautiful back-to-frontness!

Yet, nonetheless, as the apostle writes, these issues can "torment" us. It's big and it's real and it's painful.

Clinical psychologist, and a contemporary scholar on shame, Gershen Kaufman, is quoted on *Psychology Today* as saying "Shame is the most disturbing experience individuals ever have about themselves; no other emotion feels more deeply disturbing because in the moment of shame the self feels wounded from within."[9]

And because its such a disturbing experience, a "wounding within", there will be any number of emotional, physical, psychological, physiological, and spiritual reactions and responses to it. Resulting behaviours will be broad and varying. Through personal experience and years of ministry I've seen how shame can trigger behaviours and ways of coping that are painful for ourselves for and others. It's key to understand quite how damaging unaddressed shame is, either for yourself or for those around you who you are struggling. I've had more than my share of "experimenting" with coping strategies, which together we will look at in the next chapter.

9   Quoted in Jane Bolton, "What We Get Wrong about Shame", 18 May 2009 (https://www.psychologytoday.com/blog/your-zesty-self/200905/what-we-get-wrong-about-shame).

Combating shame through Scripture

It takes active work to walk in freedom from shame. One of the biggest, most robust, and therapeutic tools to assist with this is the heart-absorption of – ta-da! – God's Word, and, of course, ladlefuls of prayer.

Not just the reading of Scripture, but the type of activity where the heart actually absorbs the words. Like a poem that hits you between the eyes – your heart absorbs it; or a kind person with some positive words when you were at your lowest – your heart absorbs it; or when you see a view that takes your breath away – your heart absorbs it. That's what I mean by *reading* Scripture. Your heart absorbs it. Hebrews 4:12 explains how this dynamic is possible: "For the word of God is alive and powerful. It is sharper than the sharpest two-edged sword, cutting between soul and spirit, between joint and marrow. It exposes our innermost thoughts and desires." If we were in any doubt as to what we've just read, let's just summarize that the Word of God is alive, powerful, sharp, and exposing. There's not a lot else out there that can do that, my friends! No relationship, no drug, no bottle of Chardonnay.

One of my most favourite heart-absorbed Scriptures is Isaiah 61:1–11 – "Good News for the Oppressed":

The Spirit of the Sovereign Lord is upon me,
for the Lord has anointed me
to bring good news to the poor.
He has sent me to comfort the brokenhearted
and to proclaim that captives will be released
and prisoners will be freed.
He has sent me to tell those who mourn
that the time of the Lord's favor has come,
and with it, the day of God's anger against their enemies.
To all who mourn in Israel,
he will give a crown of beauty for ashes,
a joyous blessing instead of mourning,
festive praise instead of despair.
In their righteousness, they will be like great oaks
that the Lord has planted for his own glory.

They will rebuild the ancient ruins,
repairing cities destroyed long ago.
They will revive them,
though they have been deserted for many generations.
Foreigners will be your servants.
They will feed your flocks
and plow your fields
and tend your vineyards.
You will be called priests of the Lord,
ministers of our God.
You will feed on the treasures of the nations
and boast in their riches.

Instead of shame and dishonour,
you will enjoy a double share of honour.
You will possess a double portion of prosperity in your land,
and everlasting joy will be yours.

"For I, the Lord, love justice.
I hate robbery and wrongdoing.
I will faithfully reward my people for their suffering
and make an everlasting covenant with them.
Their descendants will be recognized
and honoured among the nations.
Everyone will realize that they are a people
the Lord has blessed."

I am overwhelmed with joy in the Lord my God!
For he has dressed me with the clothing of salvation
and draped me in a robe of righteousness.
I am like a bridegroom dressed for his wedding
or a bride with her jewels.
The Sovereign Lord will show his justice to the nations of
the world.
Everyone will praise him!
His righteousness will be like a garden in early
spring, with plants springing up everywhere.

As a fairly long in the tooth Christian, I've heard many (if not preached them) sermons on Isaiah 61 … and the primary focus leans toward encouraging mission: preaching good news to the poor and broken-hearted and freeing the captives. Wonderful!

But, this text is much richer than a first read may suggest. It's a beautiful pledge of restoration to those who "mourn" and looks to a promised new covenant with God – with the prophet's conclusion being to rejoice at God's actions.

Interestingly, I identify myself as the person who mourns as readily as I see myself as the missionally minded "preacher of good news". Do you? Mourning the loss of unborn children, mourning reputation because something's not worked out, mourning the death of dear ones, mourning not finding a passionate or committed partner, mourning a dream, mourning being able to be fully free emotionally…

And Isaiah 61 has some powerful words for those who mourn… for me… and for you: "Instead of shame and dishonour you will enjoy a double share of honour. You will possess a double portion of prosperity in your land, and everlasting joy will be yours."

I've heart-absorbed this Scripture over and over! It declares not just that shame and dishonour will be soothed, or neutralized, or even eradicated… no, instead to whatever measure of shame and dishonour there was, a double portion's worth of it will be enjoyed in the form of honour, prosperity (not the tanned TV evangelist "loads of cash be yours" version but the "I'm settled, stable, rooted, flourishing in a God-given place" version), and everlasting joy. Everlasting joy. Yes please, I'll have that. As British as I am, my reserve goes when the reality of this Scripture takes hold; I want to dance and whoop, "Bring it on!"

Reading Scriptures has reshaped my thinking on so many levels. There's nothing else I can be shaped by more, and *want* to be shaped by more. No person, guru, or experience. Romans 12:2 reads "Don't copy the behavior and customs of this world, but let God transform you into a new person by changing the way you think. Then you will learn to know God's will for you, which is good and pleasing and perfect."

And changing our thinking is what is going to stop shame engulfing us with its secrets and lies and what will allow us to be transformed into people who live to their God-given potential. The very essence of kindsight is about thinking differently. With kindness we can replace condemnation, and with embracing and learning we can replace our mentally beating ourselves up.

Managing painful memories

There is many a time when a painful memory shuttles at high speed back into my consciousness – most of the time being something I would prefer not to recall; be it a personal failing or a shaming experience. The memory actually arrests me for a wee second, and then a physical cringe ripples through my body – and I can feel literally shaken at the memory; at times breathless, remembering the shame felt at that moment, even if it was years or decades back. Can you relate to this? It's like reliving it all over again.

One memory came flooding into my mind only the other day, and it produced a shame-induced shudder! It goes something like this. Some years ago now, I was on a particularly interesting senior team (for the sake of honouring all involved, I'll leave the defining features of the story vague). One person who was known for their autocratic leadership style, decided that certain people did not support them enough, or didn't fit the bill any more, or were being too challenging of their decisions, and summarily dismissed, with immediate effect, the staff to whom they felt this applied. Including me. With no warning – just a letter.

The wider leadership body, already dealing with a multitude of challenging issues and areas of fall-out, were becoming exasperated, and were all tired. There was no template in the handbook as to how to deal with yet another bizarre and irrational scenario. What was I to do? Fight this leader's actions, write a letter demanding an apology, or just accept it and be relieved that I was better off being out of what was a very tricky situation? I didn't fight it. I just wrote a counter-letter of resignation. It was posted and I limped off home. The wrong decision even to this day. Even though I knew "the dismissal" wasn't actually personal, as I was but one in a long line of casualties, I went into meltdown, privately. Externally I clung to dear, faithful, and loyal friends who saw and felt the injustice of the situation. They quickly pulled me through into a far brighter new day with gusto. But for that meltdown moment, internally, I felt like a teenager again, transported back to a time when I couldn't process the emotions, where I felt embarrassed and maligned.

So on the day, recently, when the memory of getting the dismissal letter came at me full throttle, I chose to sit down with it in true kindsight fashion, and instead of cringing and distracting myself until it went away, I invited it to take a chair at the kitchen table. Yes, I offered it a seat. And I spoke to it. And told it I wanted to learn from it. Even though I felt physically and emotionally uncomfortable, I harnessed this moment. I realized I could change my thinking about the memory as much as I've learned it's possible to do this about every negative statement that enters our heads.

So there, at the table, I addressed the memory. By speaking aloud (the flat was empty!) and honestly about my recollections, I was able to work through the incident. I now with kindsight recognize the following:

- A shame-filled "wounding within" had occurred, which is why it was excruciating for me.

- The false belief system came into play that there was something inherently "wrong with me" rather than something being wrong with the situation.

- At the time, instead of being able to see the situation for what it was, I could only translate the event through unresolved previous shame-encounters of times when I had failed at something close to my heart, which this particular organization and people within it, were. Hence, I went from confident, strategic, impactful leader to crushed individual in a day.

- This prevented me from assessing the situation in not only being able to see the wood for the trees, but it stopped me from taking responsibility for where I perhaps hadn't dealt with this individual's working style well and had allowed tensions to build.

- The simple analysis is that some of my actions had tapped into this leader's general insecurities and I became a casualty of that.

- And the reason why I didn't interpret it as such then and therefore didn't have the tenacity to eyeball the situation with a steely glare – was that at this point in my emotional evolving, resident shame prevented me.

The kitchen had been party to a peace treaty between me and something that had had the ability to still unsettle me. Calm entered my body and mind. And, for the first time, I felt this "dismissal" incident and I had integrated. I no longer felt a "cringe", nor a remorse. Even though I'd forgiven the individual a long time ago, the incident had admittedly sat painfully in the background over the passing years. But now, I felt differently: resigned, settled, contented. I wasn't in denial; the incident had still happened, the pain had still occurred, the shame had still won back then. But, by dealing with the memory, I had finally stopped beating myself up, and I had actually learned something from the experience. I embraced the pain, acknowledged it, reflected upon, and took ownership of my contribution. I owned *it* now. It didn't own me.

What painful memory might you invite to the table? And choose to learn from instead of run away from? Perhaps a failed relationship still irks you and you feel either still very much the victim or shame at how you treated someone? Or have you likewise had a tough experience at work, a redundancy, non-promotion, or a dismissal? Whichever it is, this kindsight exercise will help the negative experience to be integrated and will give you an opportunity to learn something about yourself that you might not have seen before. And when that happens, something good can flow. And we grow. And shame has less impact than it did before. Transformation is at play.

Thank you, God.

4

On Coping Strategies that Hurt and Forgiveness that Heals

Life throws us all curveballs. I haven't yet met one person who hasn't experienced some form of trauma or negative experience. And neither have I ever met anyone who has walked through that trauma with not a blip on their emotional heartbeat monitor. In fact, were they to have done so, it would have made them a waxwork model: lifeless and emotionally devoid.

Negative coping strategies

Having zero reaction to the tough stuff of life is more unhealthy than someone who openly registers pain, hurt, anger, frustration, sadness, or grief – all of which are appropriate and healthy responses when we're going through trauma. However, when such responses don't have a constructive exit route upon having served their purpose, they can become destructive rather than helping us to heal.

And once they've nestled into our souls, we can develop negative coping strategies to deal with these very responses that were, in the first instance, a natural part of recognizing and dealing with trauma. Grief, for example, cannot be avoided when we encounter a loss. To feel it, is to work through it, is to be able to accept the loss, is to heal. But if we get stuck at "to feel it" and don't move on from there, the chances are we will find something else to help us cope with living in the pain of the loss. And this rarely helps.

A booklet available on mindfuloccupation.org shares that "Coping strategies can be both constructive/adaptive or destructive/maladaptive. Maladaptive coping skills are ways of dealing with stress that usually make things worse."[10]

There was a time when the way I dealt with pain and stress did indeed just make things worse. My life before faith and Bible college was very corporate, including as it did shoulder pads, monthly savings targets, and high levels of competition. And, the majority of my friendships within this corporate world were superficial and inconsistent, with the exception of a few. My day-to-day friendships typically centred around socializing and drinking; these friends were, however, easy company and the friendships at least happy ones. But life was stressful. The job I had as a buyer meant I had to save the company thousands of pounds a month by reducing how much the business spent but yet ensuring product quality and value were maintained. The travel was relentless. Numerous romantic liaisons ended without my being overly concerned, which is more worrying than them having mattered to me. I had become numb. There wasn't an ounce of kindsight known to me.

10   Mindful Occupation, *Rising Up without Burning Out*, 2012, from chapter 7, "Coping Skills in Times of Stress" (http://mindfuloccupation. org/coping-skills-in-times-of-stress/).

By this point in my life my destructive coping mechanisms and strategies were deeply ingrained. The perception of a lack of family love in my childhood years had left a void – an emotional canyon – which I would tumble into regularly. The long and exhausting climb out became tedious and all too common. I was tired of it all myself. Dog tired in fact. Sad thing to say about one's twenties.

Add that to life's pressures such as work, paying bills, managing a variety of relationships, the quest for "happiness"… In the end I found ways that I thought were helping me to cope. But in fact they did the exact opposite. Mine were:

1. Coping strategy #1: I would drink too much to attempt to curb low-level anxiety and avoid the pervading sense that I wasn't loveable.

2. Coping strategy #2: I would have sex with too many men in an attempt to break through the emotional numbness built up over the years. The reality was that I just wanted to be held, loved, adored, and to share life meaningfully with someone.

3. Coping strategy #3: I would flex my personality to blend into circumstances so I could fit in. It wasn't so much being a people-pleaser as watching the scene and those around me, tuning into their ideologies and assertions – and reflecting back to them those particular things, but as though they were mine.

There are countless other coping strategies. Do you recognize yourself in the ones above, or in some of the more commonly seen strategies below? Take some time to sit and think on this. Perhaps this might be your moment of revelation, to accept that you're using a coping strategy in life that is now causing pain as opposed to aiding you.

Withdrawal from people, from family, from the world. The perceived benefit to the individual is that they don't have to share or explain the feelings of pain that they are feeling. Withdrawal removes the threat that people might find out about things we wish to keep hidden. The challenge is that isolation and loneliness can take a deep hold. Depression, once isolated, is more likely to develop. This simply compounds the negative feelings of self in the first instance. Oftentimes, withdrawal (whereby there is a conscious shift from being socially engaged to being socially isolated as a coping strategy) can be confused with introversion (a natural temperament). However, I've witnessed people who have consciously withdrawn return to their natural personality type once they have shared their difficulties: they can once again be replenished by the company of others and enjoy new group activities.

Putting on a false front. This could be by being overly nice (please like me), self-sacrificing (I'll put your needs first to encourage you to like me), being a "hyper" version of self (I'll win you over with attention and/or my engaging personality), or, as I shared earlier, flexing one's own natural personality to try and fit in. Therefore an individual operating within this coping mechanism can develop an external persona that is different from that of their private self. This persona is intended to convince others of their general well-being, likeability, and an "all's OK with the world". It's largely a distraction technique for both themselves and others from seeing the sadness, loneliness, and pain of the present, for example, "If I show you how pleasant I am, how happy I am to put your needs first, if I show you how much I'm enjoying life, then you will never know the pain I feel. For you to know would be to compound my pain." Oftentimes this maladaptive coping mechanism can be extremely tiring as it requires a huge effort to maintain this persona when the heart is feeling so different from the projection.

Self-harming. This is sadly becoming more and more commonplace. It's another way that people with acute emotional pain cope. Self-harming tends to be a private, ritualistic activity, where the individual expresses tangibly their self-loathing, shame, repressed trauma, or, in some cases, the anger they feel toward people or situations they feel have negatively impacted them. The act itself is intended to relieve the emotional pressure felt, or indeed make a physical "mark" in order to feel that the emotional pain has been recognized. Due to the chemicals released during the harming – through pain, through euphoria, through accomplishment, and through "release" – the brain produces endorphins which cause a temporary sense of well-being. And so the feeling of well-being, albeit secured at a high cost, becomes embedded in the psyche as an addiction of sorts. To feel "better" about oneself in "that moment" when feelings become unmanageable, self-harming becomes compulsive.

And as with all addictions, nothing ultimately gets solved (that is, it's a destructive coping mechanism, not a constructive one). In fact, as with most addictions, shame gets compounded – due to the "irrational" nature of the act, the physical scarring, the embarrassment of others finding out, and the very real issue of oftentimes being unable to stop.

Ingesting substances that alter mood. Drugs, alcohol, and food are the most popular means of altering one's mood. The use of drugs and alcohol is largely about simply trying to feel better by chemically changing the way we feel. However, all in this list are highly addictive and none bring any short-, mid-, or long-term benefits to the person.

- **Alcohol**. The plain facts are that ethanol (the active ingredient in alcohol) changes our mood, the chemicals in our body, and alters our "normal" self. For me, alcohol became a coping mechanism in that I wanted to secure that feeling of relaxation, to dull memories, and avoid things I couldn't otherwise put out of my mind – in other words, I wanted to park some of the difficult stuff that was going on, if only for a few hours. In and of itself, nothing wrong with those desires. Yet, the next morning still came, the mind was still active on those difficult issues that were there the day before, and all that was achieved was a lighter purse, an unnecessary 1,000-calorie intake, and a fuzzy morning head that took a good shower and several aspirins to dissipate. Not huge rewards!

- At the time of writing this book I'm currently fasting alcohol, as I have done previous times, as a personal discipline in my life. Three specific times I can remember previously are: first, fasting for three years when at Bible College and then on into ministry; second, when I was setting up a community home to foster homeless teenagers and for the first year of its running; and third, when contemplating IVF and in preparation for it (though the IVF programme never commenced). This fourth time round, I'm abstinent because there are some current challenging personal situations I'm trying to walk through with wisdom, confidence, and dignity. During a time of prayer I felt that God wanted me to have no distractions: for me to be fully and utterly present. For me to emotionally feel everything has been of the utmost importance – to not dull anything. God has needed me to have "laser-like" focus on certain goals so I could orient this season well. Not least writing my first book. Might God be whispering (or yelling!) to someone reading this right now? Are you feeling a nudge to be abstinent for a season, to fast alcohol in order to regain full clarity in life and put Him first? If today is the day, then make it the day. Grab this moment, and run toward the challenge if you feel God is prompting you to give up alcohol. You'll know. (Two superb books to aid abstinence are Allan Carr's *Easy Way to Control Alcohol* and, specifically for women, *The Sober Revolution* by Sarah Turner and Lucy Rocca.)

- **Drugs**. These substances are no different from alcohol, inasmuch as the aim of taking them is to alter mood. The effects of taking legal, illegal, or prescribed drugs range enormously. As does the social taboo and ultimate "life-impact", as regular drug users will attest to. Sadly, for some, it's not long before the addiction is life-controlling. And what accompanies that is more and more money being required to fund the addiction (of course, no different with alcohol); the loss of interest in much else so full focus can be given to the addiction (as becomes the need to alter mood); and the reduction in competencies and ability to hold things together. Worst case scenario, this can result in loss of family, reputation, finance, home, and career.

- **Food**. This is a complicated one. Our bodies need neither alcohol nor drugs, but we all need food. The use of food as a coping mechanism can be seen in conditions such as binge-eating, bulimia, and anorexia. The most common coping strategy in regard to food, however, would probably be "emotional eating": the compulsion to eat at times of general anxiety, when angry or sad or lonely. It creates a psychological and physiological reliance on food for emotional coping.

High performance, achievement, power. It goes without saying that many high achievers can simply be individuals with drive, tenacity, and a competitive bent. We need these people in the world to get things done! However, I've met as many with these traits who consciously or subconsciously are "covering up" emotional pain or over-compensating for their "perceived" inadequacies. This is often a complicated coping mechanism, as there are often tangible benefits surrounding the behaviour that compound the coping mechanism. A friend from the past was a business owner, having built the business from scratch, and within a few years was making a significant amount of money. Attached to running a successful marketing company was a prestige and a sense of power. On the one hand this provided my friend with big cars and big houses, both of which were markers of "social success", as was the credibility that running a business brought with it. However, beneath it all was someone who was racked with insecurity. And dysfunction. Having grown up in an abusive parent–child relationship the majority of relationships they entered failed because they didn't know how to love themselves. Yet, even against that backdrop of pain, externally they were deemed successful by the society around them.

Projecting blame. We learn to do this from a very early age. We've all seen examples of children in the playground who immediately point to another kid when they're busted on something they shouldn't have been doing: "It wasn't me, it was him!" Even if they are caught red-handed they simply deny blame. This behaviour is often motivated by the need to avoid disapproval, or avoid consequences, and it is not uncommon that they might want to preserve their self-image as a "good" boy or girl. We seemingly often don't grow up in this area. I know many adults whose behaviour is still motivated in the same way! Many of us are still motivated by the need to avoid disapproval, avoid consequences, and preserve self-image. Sadly, for some of us, it's precisely because we received so much disapproval in our lives from key attachment figures or within the education system, that we developed the coping mechanism of projecting blame, simply in order to live with ourselves. To have absorbed the blame, be it warranted or not, would have meant taking on too much shame. And so we learned how to deflect away from ourselves. Particularly worrying is when this becomes a subconscious rather than a conscious choice.

American psychologist Albert Ellis nailed it when he addressed this very issue. "The best years of your life are the ones in which you decide your problems are your own. You do not blame them on your mother, the ecology, or the president. You realize that you control your own destiny." By blaming others, we are in fact giving away the power to change. And power to change ourselves for better is one of the most poignant defining factors of being human versus that of simply being a living organism.

Sex. In an age where any sexual appetite can be fed with a £20 note or a laptop, and with little social stigma, it's easy to see why sexual compulsions have had the gate of opportunity opened up to them. Casual sex; illicit sex; purchased sex; forced sex; child sex; porn sex; in-the-mind sex; solo sex; orgy sex; anonymous-in-the-public-toilets sex… all this goes on day after day after day. In cities, towns, and villages. Sex at its best and within good and helpful parameters is wonderful, liberating, and stress-busting. No wonder then that, being this good, the enemy of the age has turned it into a distorted, cracked image of what it should be. What probably starts off for most people as a distraction tool, a bit of light relief, a coping method for managing some anxiety or hurt – in the form of using porn, or having casual sex because it glinted at the prospect of being held for a night – turned, however slowly, into sexual compulsions that now chain and oppress. Sex, one of God's greatest inventions, has sadly become one of life's most destructive coping mechanisms.

It would be very easy at this point to feel down and disheartened, particularly if this chapter so far has struck a painful chord. With true kindsight, instead of beating ourselves up, or – worse still – judging others, the greatest gift we can give is compassion. Compassion will have a far greater chance of combating a negative coping mechanism than condemnation ever will.

Constructive coping strategies

And let's not forget! There are multiple constructive coping strategies available to us too. From religion, to being around good people, through to tennis – there are really positive ways by which we can tackle the stresses and strains of life. My top three can be summarized as: faith, friendships, and the forgiveness of self. Three strong Fs!

Faith

Faith, for me, has been one of the greatest ways I have been able to constructively cope and thrive in life. My faith has given me purpose, a moral compass, the gift of prayer, and spiritual disciplines such as rest, silence, abstinence. An agnostic friend of mine shares with me that she finds using relaxation techniques such as meditation and calm reflection helpful. These have helped her with some compulsive behaviours that previously she was struggling to get under control.

In the 1960s Dr Herbert Benson of Harvard Medical School and the Benson-Henry Institute for Mind Body Medicine at Massachusetts General Hospital discovered the power of relaxation to reduce stress. But his subsequent research found that the approach is really no different from that which people have done for centuries – through prayer, chanting, and repetitive motion.

An article on the American Psychological Association's website goes on to say, "Today, scientists have shown that such practices lower heart rates, blood pressure and oxygen consumption, and they alleviate the symptoms associated with a vast array of conditions, including hypertension, arthritis, insomnia, depression, infertility, cancer, anxiety, even aging."[11] All this, just from the discipline of prayer! Yet more than that, prayer also helps us to go beyond ourselves, to lean on God, to know we aren't alone, and to have eternal perspective.

11   Sara Martin, "The Power of the Relaxation Response", No. 9, Vol. 39, 2008 (http://www.apa.org/monitor/2008/10/relaxation.aspx).

Without my relationship with God our Father, I would be flaying about in a vast expanse of deep, deep water with no coastline or arm bands if it weren't for His anchor. Yet it's astonishing how quickly my attention leaves God when I'm struggling. It moves swiftly on to the issue at hand, and I place all the energy I should be spending on God, instead of trying to sort out the issue I should be leaving with Him. Round and round I go, eventually ending up back at His feet again, tired but relieved I found my way back. You'd think I'd learn! What I do know is that God is cheering us on in every regard, and leaning into Him is the single most beneficial coping mechanism I have encountered.

Friendships

Second to that, and of vital importance in helping us cope with stress and trauma, is the coping mechanism encapsulated in positive, secure, mutually loving human relationships.

In today's society, particularly Western society, we have minimized the value we place on being interdependent on people. It is one of the fundamental ways, since time immemorial, that people have learned to cope with trauma and emotional pain – through the support of others. This is backed up by the Alameda County Study's results of studying 7,000 residents over thirty years, which found that the most isolated people were three times more likely to die than those who had strong support networks. As pastor, author, and speaker John Ortberg comments, "People who have bad health habits (such as smoking, poor eating habits, obesity, or alcohol use) but strong social ties live *significantly longer* than people who have great health habits but are isolated."[12]

In other words, it is better to eat Mars Bars with good friends than to eat broccoli alone. Robert Putnam notes that if you belong to no groups but then decide to join one, "you cut your risk of dying over the next year in *half*".[13] Man alive. You couldn't make this stuff up! If I join the gym, the church, and the reading club then I should be OK!

Biological evidence confirms these "connecting with others" theories. Contact with others stimulates production of the neuropeptide oxytocin, which acts as a hormone connecting with organ systems, and as a neurotransmitter that signals with the brain and throughout the autonomic nervous system. Loneliness increases the perception of stress, interferes with immune function, and impairs cognitive function, whereas oxytocin has the opposite effect. Oxytocin, which has been called the hormone of "affiliation" or "love drug", has been found to prevent detrimental cardiac responses, and is believed to underpin the link between social contact and healthy hearts. So the next time you go to email someone who's at the desk next to you, pop your head round instead!

There is something so reassuring to live in connected community, with either extended family or "family of choice" who know us and what to expect from us, love us, put up

12   John Ortberg, *Everybody's Normal Till You Get to Know Them*, Zondervan, 2003, p. 33.
13   Robert D. Putnam, *Bowling Alone: The Collapse and Revival of American Community*, Simon & Schuster, 2001, p. 331.

with us, and share the burden with us. Galatians 6:2 in the Amplified Bible says, "Bear (endure, carry) one another's burdens and troublesome moral faults, and in this way fulfill and observe perfectly the law of Christ (the Messiah) and complete what is lacking in your obedience to it." OK but only as long as you put up with troublesome moral faults in return!

Meaningful relationships in my life have been my saving grace – second only to my faith. My friendships are the single biggest source of joy and comfort I have. I'm constantly amazed at people's loyalty, commitment, and long-suffering of me. There will be rewards in heaven, all you Tarn-folk!

Forgiving self

The sources of stress and trauma are, of course, endless. We often think of trauma stemming from either something that the forces of nature have bestowed upon us, or that someone or something has caused. And this can indeed be the case. Yet, sometimes we have to live with significant consequences from trauma that are our doing and our doing alone.

I personally feel that this is sometimes harder to cope with than when something, even if horrific or unjust, happens at the hand of another or through a *force majeure*. When we are to blame, it can be unbearable. Perhaps it's because it's somehow easier, if not morally noble and dignified, to forgive another. We seem to be able to muster more compassion for others than for ourselves. Or to stoically resign ourselves to what was an unforeseeable event or accident (recognizing this too takes great character and "enlightened" soul-fibre to step into a place of acceptance and forgiveness). But to forgive oneself for an almighty self-caused-shambles, a moral failure, a betrayal toward those we claimed to love, hidden coping mechanisms that are hurting us, a secret addiction even, a tantalizingly embarrassing social failure such as getting tipsy at the vicarage tea party and falling into the prize gladioli (purely fictional, dear friends, purely fictional…). To forgive ourselves? Excuse me! Forgive ourselves? The person who least deserves it in the whole wide world? Never!

Yet to forgive oneself is one of the most ongoing constructive coping strategies I know. How many of us are walking around with stooped shoulders and a defeatist attitude because of our own failings? Lots. Even though we've repented, said sorry a million times, considered moving to the most remote, permanently inhabited, island on Earth – Tristan da Cunha; begged for mercy and researched flagellation on Google. But what is first required is the art of *self-forgiveness*! This entails standing in front of the mirror and saying something not dissimilar to "You fell on your face, my dear friend. It won't be the last time. And right now, I'm going to treat you with kindness and forgive you, because that way you can learn and try to avoid the same mistake again. Onward, old chap." I must have had a hundred of these conversations with myself over the years. Often followed by prayer that hands, rather sheepishly, the whole sorry mess over to Jesus. Again.

The sheer liberty that forgiveness of self brings is startling and life-changing. Of all the pop psychology we're bombarded with these days (not least the thousands of excellent self-help books printed every year), forgiving oneself seems to be the last bastion of collective non-discovery! Believe me, it's fundamental to being whole. And it's crucial if ever we are to truly accept ourselves, faults and all. I'm not talking here about condoning wrong behaviour, nor staying firmly in the "muddy pigpen of sin and evil intent" (I read that in a very zealous American book on evangelism the other day, and, being a pictorial kind of gal, it stuck in my head!): of course not. We all have a responsibility as Christians, and if not Christians, then as decent human beings, to step up and change the game we're playing if it's constantly destructive and less than what we can give and what others deserve.

What we're talking about here is the art of embracing personal if not painful truth and still be OK with ourselves, which we're enabled to do, through love. God's love for us, that is. And when we know that love, that perfect love, we need never have to prove anything again to anyone, nor will we believe that we will only be loved if we're perfect. Which is hogwash. Tish. Tosh. Bulldust. We are loved and loved dearly as we are, with who we are right now, bringing what we bring right now. Because of the work of the cross. The Christian faith is so profound; it teaches this:

Yet it was our weaknesses he carried;
it was our sorrows that weighed him down.
And we thought his troubles were a punishment from God,
a punishment for his own sins!
But he was pierced for our rebellion,
crushed for our sins.
He was beaten so we could be whole.
He was whipped so we could be healed.
All of us, like sheep, have strayed away.
We have left God's paths to follow our own.
Yet the Lord laid on him
the sins of us all.

Isaiah 53:4–6

He carries our weakness; He takes the weight of our sorrows; He absorbs our rebellion; He was hurt so we could hand over our sin, be made whole, and be healed. And even though we've wandered off on our own merry journey, Jesus takes the full hit for every mistake we have ever made, and will still yet ever make. Man, we're loved. We've got to get this truth deep into us. It changes everything. If this truth doesn't position us to love and respect ourselves, after someone has done this for us, I don't know what will.

It's this that aids self-forgiveness; it's this that means I can view my life with kindsight, embracing both my own, and the fears and failures of others and see them differently. We are never unredeemable or beyond the love and grace of God. Quite the opposite: He forgives, and He offers kindness. And if He forgives us everything, as far as "the east is from the west" (Psalm 103:12), it's a little conceited to imagine we can't do the same!

Self-forgiveness is to free ourselves up; it's the emancipation of guilt and shame. In Scriptural terms we need to draw down from Isaiah 61 again – this time from verse 1 – and receive the Scripture that Jesus wants to "heal the heartbroken" and "announce freedom to all captives" (MSG) (that's us!). This freedom is a gift, through Jesus, available for every single one of us, with no exceptions.

It's the holding on to guilt and shame and a lack of forgiveness that keeps many of us bound up and unable to live lightly and freely without constraint. Recently I spoke with a lady who had given up a child for adoption thirty years back. The child was a result of rape by a second cousin. She had forgiven the perpetrator of the rape years back and was able to pray for him and his family, but had never afforded herself the same forgiveness in giving the child up for adoption. We had what I call a productive "carpet-ministry" time, where, on her knees, she wailed, allowing the trauma and the pain of the non-forgiveness toward herself, to come out. Snot, tears, and years of her self-persecution were shared. And she's now walking free of guilt and forgiven. And two very significant coping strategies she had used as a crutch for many years dissipated the same day. That is not a coincidence.

How few people ever find this liberty? And as a result how many of us develop coping mechanisms that may give temporary relief, but will rarely bring the freedom we're talking about here? Too many.

Being truthful with ourselves

In the 2010 "chick flick" *Eat, Pray, Love*, Julia Roberts plays the role of Elizabeth Gilbert, on whose memoirs the film is based. In the film, Gilbert teaches us that if we embark on a truth-seeking journey, if we choose to learn from everything and everyone, if we are brave enough to forgive ourselves even on the really difficult stuff then truth will not be withheld from us.

I think there's gold dust in here. In John 8:31 Jesus says of true discipleship "… you will know the truth, and the truth will set you free." He said this just before people started throwing stones at Him (John 8:58). It was seemingly not a popular message! (Granted, Jesus was accusing them of being illegitimate children – not spiritually descending from Abraham but instead from "the dark side". Ahem!)

If we are willing to forgive some very difficult realities about ourselves, then truth is wide open to us. I want that, don't you? In order to forgive or – equally as important in kindsight philosophy – to learn those realities about ourselves, we have to be aware of them. For some this is scary and unknown territory. We beautiful humans can live quite happily in abject denial and/or convince ourselves of another truth entirely so we don't have to face facts. Denial and revisionism – the bedrock of most problems!

There are a number of realities we are all negotiating at any point in time. The ones we don't want, the ones we don't mind, the ones we revise according to how we want things to be, and the ones we want – but, importantly, there's a fifth. There are the ones we don't even know of! We're not in denial of them; we genuinely don't know what they are! Personally I really want to know about these unknown realities in my life that I can't see but others can, albeit conveyed to me gently and with a sprinkling of love-dust and humour, rather than an intense finger-wagging session called "Prayerful feedback"! Choosing to find out, accept, and embrace truth about ourselves is a significant step in being able to change the way we cope. It's empowering.

In summary, therefore, the greater the awareness we have of our true selves, and the extent to which we forgive ourselves having taken responsibility of what we find – all significantly inform the type, shape, and depth of coping mechanisms we engage when trying to cope with stress and trauma.

Keeping clean

Even once we've become aware of our coping mechanisms, found positive replacement strategies, have forgiven ourselves, and are living in truth, the battle is still on: the battle that the apostle Paul talks of in Ephesians 6:12, "For our struggle is not against flesh and blood, but against the rulers, against the authorities, against the powers of this dark world and against the spiritual forces of evil in the heavenly realms." There are powers in this world that would seek to keep us bound up in negative coping mechanisms and in places of pain and shame. By their very nature they are intent on causing chaos. And keeping us from living to our fullest potential. The minute we allow ourselves to think we've sorted it all, we're in trouble. If our strength, or lack of it, didn't keep us from harm in the first instance then it's unlikely to do so again.

I've gradually learned how to place God at the centre and to make a Him my primary constructive and adaptive coping mechanism. Even now, in my forties, the battle is still on. It takes focused effort to keep with this as my life's order and to live in freedom. God is our safe place, our refuge, our answer. It is to Him we should cling when anxiety is rising; it is from Him we should be getting more and more of our identity; it is He who can soothe our trauma through supernatural peace.

And God would want us all celebrating our freedom in Him. Full and glorious freedom. That is my prayer for us all.

5

On Falling in Love: The Pain of Again and Again

The topic of romantic relationships is never far from people's minds. It's not surprising. Unless someone has a clear "gift" of celibacy and singleness, it's fair to say that we're wired to want to be in an intimate relationship with another human being. The majority of us have a plethora of tales to tell about love and loss; dating successes and failures; and the highs and lows of both painful short-term or blissful long-term relationships, or indeed the other way round: blissful short-term or painful long-term relationships!

Romantic love

Centuries ago, institutionalized religion used to be society's main energy source for meaning and purpose; now it's romance. It is a modern phenomenon that we bank much of our happiness on, finding that right, perfectly fitting, made-specifically-for-us partner. And what sadness this can bring us when it doesn't materialize. With this romantic "expectation", either that perfect partner can't be found at all, or is found of a sorts but it transpires they're not perfectly fitting, or is ecstatically found but we realize quickly that the relationship changes across the seasons of life and we can't keep it static and therefore "perfect". And so, the disappointment felt by so many of us in this arena of love is quite overwhelming.

We've all heard people say, "I just want to feel complete". Complete? Might this indicate we perceive there to be an inherent lack in us already and that we are therefore lacking something? I find this really worrying. Believe me when I say this is not a good place to start a relationship, neither for the person needing completion nor for the partner, knowingly or unknowingly, about to try to complete the other. It is an unachievable expectation to complete another human being. Only a magnificent, supernatural, love-consumed Father God can do this for any of us.

I'm often asked the question of whether I believe in the existence of "the one"? I think probably in my younger years, I did. But now, older, greyer, armed with my experience and that of others, I'd say "the one" typically does not exist. Don't get me wrong, I'm very happy with the concept of finding one partner as opposed to multiple. With kindsight I've learned over the years that rarely is there such a thing as "the one who fits perfectly" – including me.

It takes shared values and beliefs, humour, servanthood, intentional communication, commitment, truthfulness, sacrifice, and a whole lot of hard work – by both partners – to make a monogamous and lifelong relationship work and fit well.

People of centuries past considered much more than just the romantic notion of "the one" finding the "other one" or, in simple terms, the love-joining of two people. There would be an issue first of whether faith aligned, then whether there was economic advantage by coming together, and, significantly, there would be the appreciation that families, and therefore communities, would be joining together, not just two people. This seems to be in sharp contrast to the way in which our partners are found today.

Help with finding a partner

I have regular conversations with people who are single, divorced, or widowed (and the occasional unhappily married!) about how on earth a compatible partner can be found in our individualistic, fast-paced, consumer-led society. Is there something about bringing back the ancient art of match-making? Many ancient cultures, such as the Chinese and Jewish communities, have been doing this since time began! They have wise, mature, embedded men and women in the community who go about suggesting compatibility.

One modern Western equivalent is encapsulated by the popular US TV programme *Millionaire Matchmaker*. Patti Stanger sets out to help those high-net-worth individuals who need a guiding hand to find a compatible partner. It makes fascinating watching as she coaches individuals on how to improve their chances of successfully finding "a fit". Her advice often revolves around becoming less self-centred and more considerate towards the other person, listening instead of talking, and thinking about future goals instead of just attraction. Fairly fundamental stuff, huh? This is, perhaps, a sad reflection on us all. The individuals she coaches may be hugely efficient in business, but, like many of us, stumble at the first hurdle of learning how to live successfully with others in an intimate relationship.

Whatever route we take to find a partner, what we are concluding is that there is more likelihood of success if there is a commonly understood "joint purpose" or vision together, greater than just the "love" of and for each other. This joint purpose could be almost anything (a passion to lead a church, serving the poor in an urban environment, travel, bringing up a large family, and so on), but it ensures that there's a mutual aim when it comes to making key decisions together about the direction life should take. Partnering with people with common values, aspirations, outlooks, financial goals, cultural appreciation of the other (even if they are from different backgrounds), and a mutual desire for a long-term commitment would seem to carry some huge positives.

Of course it was, and still is, so much easier to find "fitting" partners within communities that stay together not just for lifetimes, but for generations. Centuries ago, all the people concerned in "partner-finding" knew a lot more about each other than we can possibly know now in our modern, more fragmented society. In previous centuries, the couple may well even have known each other from when they were infants!

Today, however, more often than not, the potentially life-changing decision of getting involved with someone who may eventually become our spouse, is based on the limited information we have in front of us. And let's get real – that information could be heavily filtered in their favour. Or the involvement could simply be based on sexual attraction, chemistry, or emotionally-loaded-but-not-a-lot-of-substance ("I don't know why, but I just love him/her").

And that's the danger. It's not so easy to be rational about all of the "sensible stuff" once lust grabs a hold! Even a bit further down the "let's-see-how-it-goes" line, it can be hard to assess a relationship properly if you've rushed the intimacy because you may have already formed a bond and there's a sense of obligation.

My attraction for someone used to go from 0 to 100 in a nanosecond. The combination of laughter, fun, faith, conversation, and warmth has been a heady combination for me. I have found myself in situations where my "feelings" for someone were intense, but I hadn't properly analysed whether the relationship had legs, so to speak.

My way of finding safety and security has been to immediately ask friends to come alongside in the dating process. Not in a "Are you good enough for my friend?" kind of way. Just being together socially with others helps to reduce the intensity of the fledgling relationship. By involving people who love us, to join us for food, walks, and being round each other's houses, we can rely on more than just our own perspective to gauge the relationship objectively.

I knew the friends who would tell me what they really saw! In one dating "extravaganza" I was going through years ago, a friend said to me "Get this out your system, Tarn. It's no more than a bit of fun..." I was miffed at the time, but grateful later.

She was absolutely right, and in the end I'm glad I didn't invest months into a no-goer. Good friends know us and will be real about the qualities needed that we may not care to think about while in the lust stage. They'll also be able to cool-headedly assess whether "the intended" and their friend are compatible, just as my "get-him-out-of-your-system" friend did!

Love versus infatuation

I'm of the firm opinion that society at large has confused infatuation with the true and noble virtue of love. More precisely, we have confused "loving someone" with "being in love". We just don't know the difference. The latter, "being in love", which is the West's drug of choice, is about maintaining a state of ecstasy. This becomes reliant on each partner maintaining a level of euphoria for each other. Oh my! No wonder so many relationships that move to a life-commitment based on "falling in love" fail. You can no more maintain the euphoria in the long-term than maintain helium in a fast-food restaurant's balloon. Besides, this euphoria can mask deep-seated, not-at-first-obvious incompatibilities or character issues that are impossible to see while you're on an emotional high. A female friend once jokingly said to me that she felt God designed this stage of relationship in order to "kid ourselves we love that person, enough to marry them, wash their socks and bear their children and secure the next generation. By the time we've come out the trance, it's too late!" Still makes me laugh! Forgive me, men: I don't concur with her sexist overtone, but I concede her point about infatuation being a nifty way to ensure the world is populated!

Love – deep, immovable love, based on truth and sacrifice, looking to the interest of the other before self – is remarkably rare and a jewel of great price. If ever you find this with someone, keep a precious hold of it; never for one minute imagine that there's something of greater value such as ripped muscles, big breasts, money, intellect, glamour, or fame. You may never find love like it again.

Acceptance

So, even assuming we find a love-partner, let's not kid ourselves that the hard work is over. Maintaining the relationship is the real challenge! Dr John Gottman, an eminent sociologist and relationship scientist, is quoted as saying that 40 per cent of "things people do" or "annoying behaviours" will rarely change in an individual, even if they're aware of them and try to change.[14] Therefore, if we're partnered with that individual, we have a choice. Put up with it, or walk away! The problem is, if we do walk away the next person we meet is going to have their 40 per cent of "things they do" or "annoying behaviours", albeit different things. So we'd have to put up with those or, again, walk away from that person too. If it's not one thing, it'll always be another. Not to mention adding to that mix the 40 per cent

14   As stated in the podcast "The Science of Trust: Emotional Attunement for Couples", 2013 (http://www.blogtalkradio.com/thesecretlivesofmen/2012/07/03/featured-replay-the-science-of-trust-with-john-gottman).

of us that someone has to put up with! It's with kindsight that I've learned that at some point we are going to have to accept the 40 per cent and we should be mightily grateful if they return the favour!

Taking responsibility

We need to take personal responsibility and avoid outsourcing the relationship to the other party! We've spoken about this a little in the previous chapter where we discussed how important it is to take responsibility and refuse to project blame. At best, the responsibility for any relationship should be shared on a fifty-fifty basis. Research shows that most of us believe we do more than 50 per cent of the input and that the other partner does less. Possibly it's fair for both to aim at, say, what we each believe to be 60 per cent, which might mean we actually have a balance. We can't expect one party to continually put in more of the effort than the other unless there is a good reason, such as chronic illness.

The challenge is that, if we genuinely feel we are taking the lion's share, and can back it up with facts, but the other partner is not willing to step up, we can't force them to put in the required effort. As sad as it may be, we cannot change them. We can only change ourselves.

And sometimes, that's just not enough to make a relationship work. I've seen many toxic situations where one party is flogging themselves to death trying to make the relationship work, but the disinterested party gets used to the dynamic and remains dysfunctional. The committed party normalizes the partner's neglect, and continues to make all the effort. Even if they try new strategies, this will not improve the situation unless *both* parties are prepared to make changes. If only one is prepared to change, the relationship can actually become abusive. The games of power and control have a wide field to play in here.

When a relationship is broken down, the best thing we can do, even through "eyes wide shut" is to honestly appraise what went wrong. It's true kindsight philosophy that we must stop beating ourselves up, but rather breathe, and choose to learn instead without a blanket blame-approach – that it was neither our or the other person's sole fault.

I've sat with people devastated at the loss of a relationship due to infidelity and what has astounded me is that, even under those circumstances (as infidelity can't be justified), a few have actuallyhad the maturity to look back at the condition of the relationship and see what might have caused the breakdown on both sides and not just blame the offending unfaithful party. This level of self-awareness and emotional honesty will only ever aid our healing and progress toward moving on.

Loving oneself

With kindsight, we need to acknowledge that "hurting people hurt people". Those within our communities who are hurt may have little self-knowledge of the impact of their behaviours. Many don't have the tools to be able to change as they are facing issues that cloud their ability to do so. It's by no means uncommon for hurt people to have no idea what it means to love themselves, let alone others. There's often an underlying dislike of who they are, sometimes with roots in dysfunctional parent–child relationships or abusive encounters in childhood. The desperately sad thing is that someone who doesn't love themselves can't possibly love another. This is serious stuff. The **only** way to love another well is if we first love ourselves. That way our boundaries will be sound, our expectations normal, and our contribution balanced. The opposite of that is of course obvious. When one party doesn't love themselves, or the essence of who they are, relationship fallout often ensues. Boundaries are skewed, expectations are too high or too low, and sacrificial, selfless contribution is either excessively martyrish, inconsistent, or else non-existent. All of which is a disaster waiting to happen.

I dated a lovely man once: a real gent with an action-man job. I was definitely the twenty-something Jane and he was definitely the thirty-something Tarzan. Yet, interestingly, the relational dynamics were not as you would expect. Sadly, this lovely man (let's call him Tom) had been rejected by his mother, who walked out on the family when he was small. He and his brother were brought up by their loving, caring father, but all three struggled with hurt and rejection issues as a result of their mother's behaviour.

By the time I met and started dating this man, he was desperate for love. Deep love. Committed love. The sort of love that didn't leave, get bored, or turn its gaze. It quickly became evident that Tom struggled with profoundly low self-esteem and he felt that if he found a woman who loved him, both the pain of his mother-rejection and the pain of his own self-doubt would be appeased. He wanted to feel OK about himself. He wanted to be told he was loveable. What he actually most wanted, albeit he didn't know it, was for his mother to have hugged him and told him, regularly and adoringly, that he was a wonderful and loved boy. His heart was longing for this maternal acknowledgment and affirmation. This never happened, and without this affirmation growing up, he hadn't learned how to love himself, or how to place value on his own worth.

Over time, our relationship went from good to wobbly to downright dysfunctional, precisely because I couldn't soothe his aching soul, however hard I tried. His need for me to keep affirming him, to meet his emotional needs, to be both mother and lover was too intense; too much for an immature girl in her early twenties. Until he dealt with the mother-rejection, Tom wasn't going to be able to have a functional relationship with any woman. The more he "needed", the more I pulled away. The more I pulled away, the more he needed. And the self-fulfilling prophecy of "women reject me" was sadly played out yet again in his life. We broke up horribly. I can still remember him, with angst written across his face, asking me, "Did you ever love me?"... I won't share my immature response.

Loving self, and showing love to self, is fundamental to our own well-being and this directly impacts the quality of our relationships. Self-acceptance is the key to accepting another – faults and all. If we can't accept ourselves, we can't accept another. Scripture attests to this. In Ephesians 5:28 it says, "In the same way, husbands ought to love their wives as they love their own bodies. For a man who loves his wife actually shows love for himself."

Let's have a look at this with a little less focus on gender specifics: any partner who is able to show love to their spouse actually shows love for themselves. To show love for ourselves is to be secure in who we are, be able to forgive ourselves, and accept our faults and weaknesses.

Imagine, then, the opposite. A partner who doesn't show love to their spouse is unlikely to show love to themselves. And if we do not love ourselves, really loving another is impossible. They are inextricably entwined. If we are insecure, unable to forgive and can't accept who we are – that's exactly how we'll love.

That needs some quality reflection! How well do we love ourselves?

If we know ourselves, are happy with the basic content of our souls, and if we're able to give ourselves a good old metaphorical hug, then we're on our way to being able to love another well.

Talking of "loving well" – or not as the case may be – there's a fascinating study that's been undertaken by Dr John Gottman, world-renowned for his work on marital stability and divorce prediction. For over thirty-five years he has undertaken innovative research with thousands of couples and has scientifically determined that there are four elements that, if found active in a relationship, can predict divorce as accurately as up to 94 per cent. He calls them the "Four Horsemen of the Apocalypse". They are:

1. Criticism. Berating our partner's achievements, personality, or character. It might sound something like "you always…"; "you never…"; "you're the type of person who…"; "why are you so …".

2. Contempt. Belittling our partner's sense of self with name-calling, non-affirming "humour", sarcasm, or mockery.

3. Defensiveness. Seeing oneself as the victim, justifying everything, refusing to hear possible truth, constantly making excuses such as "it's not my fault"; "I didn't", instead of taking responsibility for our contribution.

4. Stonewalling. Emotional and verbal distancing from the relationship by using stony silence, grunts, changing the subject, walking out or "sending someone to Coventry".[15]

It seems remarkable, doesn't it, that by **avoiding** these four traits, we could be saving our marriages. According to the Office of National Statistics, 42 per cent of marriages in England and Wales fail.[16] Just as I typed that last word "fail", an email pinged

15   John M. Gottman, *The Seven Principles for Making Marriage Work*, Harmony, 1999, p. 27ff.
16   Office for National Statistics, "What percentage of marriages end in divorce?", 9 February 2013 (http://www.ons.gov.uk/ons/rel/vsob1/divorces-in-england-and-wales/2011/sty-what-percentage-of-marriages-end-in-divorce.html).

up from a wonderful girl-friend. She and her husband run a great church but sadly her email referenced the challenge of marital breakdown. "We've had several marriages fall apart in just the last few weeks," she wrote. Marital breakdown is no respecter of anyone, even if they sit in a pew on a Sunday morning or wholeheartedly love Jesus. It can happen to us all, including those of us who could never imagine it would.

Many of us, I'm sure, will be fascinated with the "Four Horsemen of the Apocalypse". The "do not dos" are neither complicated to understand nor difficult to identify, but I know from personal experience that they are extremely hard to keep out of our relationships. It is not as simple as just don't do it! You could try an experiment, just for a week. In your primary love-relationship, be acutely aware of criticism, contempt, defensiveness, and stonewalling. Write down your results. Be honest. And see by the end of one week how you're faring! When I tried it criticism and defensiveness were the two that I clocked up most. I surprised myself by how many times I began a sentence with "I can't believe you've ..." and "Really? If only you'd ..." Gulp. It's not for the faint-hearted. But self-awareness is the key to change.

However, it may be too late for some relationships. As much as I'm a firm believer in miraculous turnarounds, I know all too well that some things can't be patched up together again for all sorts of reasons. But with kindsight we can at least learn from what has not worked – however painful.

When a relationship is successful we rarely focus on why. We just accept it and enjoy. It's when it goes wrong that we're faced with the task of processing the trauma, unpacking it, and, God-willing, trying to move forward.

We're all going to have different responses to this. The top three typical responses are:

A. acute navel-gazing and over-analysis of the how and whys

B. open honest appraisal

C. denial and avoidance: it was all "their" fault after all.

As (B) would suggest, a balanced, honest approach is the most fruitful, both in terms of being able to see the "wood for the trees", and truthfully understanding what's happened and why. Then of course there's the task ahead of accepting that the relationship is over (if reconciliation isn't deemed to be the best or safest route forward). If our tendency is either (A) or (C), then accepting the situation and moving on becomes nearly impossible. Therefore we can remain stuck and repeat the same mistakes in our next relationship. However disheartened we may or may not be, the most important thing is to stay focused on the important stuff. It's very easy when things go wrong to pick up on the small inconsequential issues and focus on *consequences* rather than the *causes*. But this simply keeps us from facing reality. By focusing on consequences, we lose the ability to look at what we ourselves may have contributed to the breakdown, and so we don't learn the lessons. Granted, when causes are gargantuan – infidelity, financial deceit, or addictions – it's very difficult to focus the mind into an analytical place. This is particularly difficult when betrayal, social stigma, children, money, and heartbreak are involved. But ultimately, by focusing on consequences we will delay our ability to understand things, accept the situation, move on, and grieve well.

Kindsight therefore encourages us to focus on the causes instead of the consequences, and by taking responsibility for our "part", however small or significant, we learn from the experience, which gives us the power to move on with congruence.

It's important to keep our hearts open to others even if we are hurting; be honest with ourselves; and work on forgiving whatever we perceive has been done to us, while forgiving ourselves for the hurt we've caused them.

The point of this book is to learn from what has happened before with kindness. We can all look back, learn, and then move forward with acceptance and healing in our hearts. That way, regardless of our relationship failures in the past, or whether we're attempting to make one work right now, we can make a difference to our future attitudes and relationship styles.

To give relationships the best chance, we need to be intentional, use huge amounts of kindsight, and deposit good things into the bank of Love by practising helpful relationship skills. Some of my favourites come again from Dr John Gottman, who has developed nine specific skills. His list covers nine skills that we can all learn and build into our relationships – including such areas as expressing appreciation, choosing to take a positive approach, trusting one another, being commited to the relationship and managing conflict.[17]

17   The full list is known as The Gottman Method for Healthy Relationships, and can be found on the website of The Gottman Foundation: http://www.gottman.com/about-gottman-method-couples-therapy.

They are a terrific instruction list.

The Bible completely underpins all the values Gottman articulates. Ephesians particularly is filled with huge wisdom on this topic, though to avoid any doctrinal arguments, I have to say, I tend to read it through a non-gender-specific lens and apply it to both husband and wife.

It talks so powerfully of what it looks like to love our partner well… Are you ready? It's quite challenging!

Here's Ephesians 5:33 from the Amplified translation:

However, let each man of you [without exception] love his wife as [being in a sense] his very own self; and let the wife see that she respects and reverences her husband [that she notices him, regards him, honours him, prefers him, venerates, and esteems him; and that she defers to him, praises him, and loves and admires him exceedingly].

My, my, my. Let's just list those again:

- To respect,
- To reverence,
- To notice,
- To regard,
- To honour,
- To prefer,
- To venerate,
- To esteem,

- To defer,
- To praise,
- To love,
- To admire exceedingly.

I've neither received nor given to someone the entirety of this list. Have you? I recall giving one or two, even three, for a period of time. What's more likely for most of us is that we trial them! And then frustration kicks in: perhaps the bin wasn't taken out, or we felt offended by something they did, and the above virtues are be withdrawn. On a good day forgiveness may be extended, and we then offer out a few more virtues, dependent on how we feel we are being treated and whether they deserve it or not! What a complicated set of subconscious negotiations! I read and re-read this Scripture regularly and have often used it in ministry settings to inspire and motivate those in relationships to understand God's heart for how we treat each other. This list can, of course, be applied to all our relationships, not just romantic. I would want my dad, for example, to say of me that I emulate these toward him.

(I took a gulp then as I re-read the list again! – some work to be done.)

As a fitting place to conclude this chapter let's contemplate the apostle Paul's words in Philippians 3:12–16:

> *I don't mean to say that I have already achieved these things or that I have already reached perfection. But I*

press on to possess that perfection for which Christ Jesus first possessed me. No, dear brothers and sisters, I have not achieved it, but I focus on this one thing: Forgetting the past and looking forward to what lies ahead, I press on to reach the end of the race and receive the heavenly prize for which God, through Christ Jesus, is calling us. Let all who are spiritually mature agree on these things. If you disagree on some point, I believe God will make it plain to you. But we must hold on to the progress we have already made.

We must hold on to the progress we have already made! With kindsight, let us do that. Whether we see our relationship history thus far as an abject failure, or whether we're doing OK – any learning is progress, regardless of where we find ourselves, if we so choose to see it like that. We can either take the lessons, forgive ourselves, forgive others, and look to what lies ahead. Or we can choose to remain in the past. I know what is more likely to bring benefit to my life and yours! Here's to being in the race together!

6

On Sex: The Good, the Bad, and the Average

I study sexuality and sexual expression a lot as a result of my experiences and those of countless others whom I have had the privilege of ministering to. I'm neither a sex-fantasist, nor a sex-toy-wielding-therapist, just a rather fascinated interpreter trying to help both myself and others orientate through the maze of sex and sexuality. A few years back, I went on holiday. Most people take the latest autobiography on holiday with them, or a *Lonely Planet* guide. But I enjoy podcasts. I was by the pool at a beautiful agriturismo in Tuscany, with multiple podcasts on sex and sexuality to hand. It was a small pool, very swanky, every recliner used up by classy, tanned Italians as opposed to white polka-dot bikini-clad Brits with luminous flip-flops (the latter was just me.)

With my headphones firmly stuck in my ears, holding on to my iPad (in a clear sandwich bag in case anyone were to splash it – classy!), I was relishing the fifty podcasts to work through in two weeks (some of whose theology I passionately contested, others that I whooped in agreement with, quietly!). I scrolled through to find a juicy one, and clicked on "play". No sound came out. I fiddled and fussed, turned buttons on and off for some while, until I realized I hadn't put the connector into the iPad, and so, at full volume, around an intimate but packed pool I was sharing "Welcome, this is John Daugherty, coming to you with a podcast for the sexually addicted, sexually broken and for those needing healing from same-sex attraction."[18] I struggled to make eye contact with my co-sunbathers for the entire rest of the holiday. All in the name of research, indeed.

I appear to be one of those people whom others feel they can talk to. People tend to talk to me about sex in a way that estate agents get approached about house prices. Or doctors get shown an abscess of the armpit at dinner parties. Or IT geeks at church get asked about fixing the laptop.

Once I was asked about the benefits of love-swings (a swing to have sex in for those of you wondering! It's not a quaint garden hammock for two!), at a Christian conference as I was pushing the pram with my two babies, as they were then. And whether I considered that, for the means of supporting the back, one was worth the investment. I smiled and encouraged its procurement.

But really, I don't mind; I'd prefer to have conversations with people that make a difference in their lives rather than just making small talk about the weather. And sex is one of the least talked about-most consequential activities known to mankind. Of course, I mean "talked about" as in meaningful conversation, not talked about as in smutty jokes,

18   For those who are interested, it was John Daugherty's podcast "What do you believe?" http://www.sermonaudio.com/sermoninfo. asp?SID=42115166290.

Page 3 write-ups, XXX-rated channels, and so on. We talk more about our bowel health than we do about our sexual well-being – and I don't mean who's off down the clinic for a dose of antibiotics and a packet of free condoms. Instead I mean discussion on our sexual expression, appropriate management of it, techniques, thankfulness, disappointment – and on it goes.

My regular research and contemplation on the issue of sex has led me to believe that out of all the design intelligence showcased by our Creator, sex, and reproduction in general, has to be up there with the most intriguing! He designed fantastically innovative bits in and on these bodies and sensual parts that when "this gets touched here and here, and this goes there and there and there – voila!", it bring bliss and more. It could have been designed with no more than function in mind, but then with no pleasure involved, would we go to all the effort of getting messy?!

Skip past this paragraph now if you have a sensitive disposition (it's amazing you've made it this far if you are! My prayers are with you!). It's genuinely interesting to me then as to why all the sex bits are within such close proximity or directly cofunctioning alongside poo and wee, farts, periods, and birth. I suspect it's to do with the need for us to see past these things and focus on the mind, spirit, and soul of the lover.

Sex is certainly not for the faint-hearted. It has a life force all of its own. It requires technique ("I wish!", some of you may be quietly musing!). It is a complicated mishmash of the not-so-easy and the extremely delightful.

Sex is something we can't perhaps ever fully understand; I think perhaps it's meant to have some mystique and non-containment about it.

Sex is different every time; it incites primal responses in the most stoic of us, or indeed no response in the most effusive of us. It changes as we change, both with the seasons of life and as we develop spiritually and emotionally.

Sex is intended to be a joy and a blessing to the human race; in the right hands it's a very life-affirming, satisfying activity.

Sex is also controversial, particularly the moral aspect of it in the Christian world. It's a matter of great debate: its rights, wrongs, abuse of it, abuse of others through it, our inability to handle it, or understand it.

This chapter isn't intended to be a theological treaty of the scriptural teachings on sex. Rather, a candid look at how the average Christian orients their way through some of the pitfalls and joys – with an aim to making things a little less taboo and seen through kindsight. My own experience and those of many hundreds of people I've ministered to over the years has taught me that sex is powerful. When it all goes well it is a beautiful expression of love and connection, and has the capacity to provide enormous emotional and physical pleasure, but its capacity to cause emotional and spiritual pain is also staggering.

And when we get it wrong, the condemnation and shame we feel is immense. Sex, when not being used for good and right purposes, can usher shame into the room almost faster than anything else. It can feel like an aching, embarrassing, gnawing sense of "badness" that needs emotional and spiritual surgery to deal with it.

Have you encountered this? Sadly, most people have. Perhaps you intended to put boundaries around sexual activity until "the right one" came along and instead have found yourself giving away a precious thing to someone who then let you down? Or you simply felt pressured. Or in many cases, the gift of our sexual self is given to someone who we thought we did love, only to find to our dismay we had made an error of judgment and the love wasn't love, but rather being in love with being in love.

Or are you dealing with shame because, while in a committed relationship, you've had – or are having – a sexual encounter with another person, or are involved in a sexual scene that isn't honouring, such as the use of porn, webcam sex, orgies, or the like? Often when in these "illicit" situations the euphoria eventually wears off, as does the excitement or mystique, and what remains is a double whammy of shame: you will then need to deal not only with managing personal shame, but also the guilt of betraying a loved one, however much one might repress or justify it.

And if that isn't enough, oftentimes we have to negotiate the condemnation of others if our "misguided" or "sinful" activities become publicly known. There's nothing some folk get more animated about than someone's latest moral failure. It seems to appeal to our human nature to be interested – perhaps it makes us feel more superior, or perhaps it deflects ourselves and others from our own sexual "plank in the eye".[19] Let's instead, just you and me, use kindsight and keep a lookout for protecting each other's failures where appropriate. Life is tough even without wider condemnation, as often our own battering ram of condemnation is a cruel enough thing. God knows it all. And He is still holding his arms out to people. *Nothing can separate us from the love of God*,[20] friends – nothing.

Common areas of guilt and shame

Sexual brokenness is a playing ground for heartache, which is why we need to tackle it together, openly and honestly. Regardless of what's happened, or how we may have let ourselves and others down, tomorrow is a new day. Full of new mercies. And, if we allow ourselves, a large dose of kindsight. Beating ourselves up only pushes us underground. We must see the failure through a lens of learning. Then we make the failure work for us by changing how we do things for the future through what we've learned. God's intention isn't that we stumble and fall and never get up, thinking that by staying down we're appropriating self-punishment effectively. It's the opposite. God needs us up on our feet. We need to dust ourselves off, take seriously our failure in order to realign our values back to Him, then ask for guidance and grace, asking forgiveness, not just of God, but of our own self, then of others. The failure now might work in our favour, as we're wiser, more

19   See Matthew 7:5.
20   Reference to Romans 8:38.

humble, and have experienced grace. Now that's a good place to be as an authentic Christian.

All but a very small minority of us have a sexual history, and one that we wouldn't want out on general release. People don't believe me when I say that. They assume they are the perverted, crass, broken anomaly and everyone else in their church or faith community is zipped up tight with willpower and holiness. It's just not the case. Don't get me wrong, I wish the picture did look different at times, yet I recognize that this area of sexuality is a deep and complex one and, for time immemorial, we humans haven't always been good at charting its choppy waters.

The "beginnings" book of Genesis alone is a riot of dubious sexual activity. A naked Noah, a lustful Pharaoh, Abram sleeping with the staff, a sordid situation in Sodom, an incestuous Lot, the rape of Dinah, Reuben and Judah both having casual sex… and that's just in one book of the Bible! As I say, even since the beginning of human history we just don't seem to be able to steward this gift of sex altogether well. But that doesn't mean we should give up trying! God wants us at our best, and, to be at our best, we need to make choices that reflect the nature and character of God. Purity, loving sacrificially, and exercising self-control would take us all a very long way in the right direction.

While it is key to take responsibility, and not sit and wallow in negative, repetitive sexual encounters, it's also important with kindsight not to beat ourselves up over our sexual history. Rather, we should take notes, take a deep breath, and establish where we want to be headed, be that with some fresh theological perspectives, be that with refining our own sexual ethic, or humbly asking God for forgiveness where we've not valued or stewarded this extraordinary gift of sex well. Negative soul-ties (that is, the very powerful bond existing between two people, discussed further on pages 130–31) in particular do need some spiritual attention, inasmuch as that some intentional prayer ministry is likely to help in order to cut the ties so we're free from those connections. To recognize that sex is as much a spiritual encounter with someone as it is a physical encounter is a milestone in itself for some and can often help in ensuring that a greater importance is placed on the sexual union from here on in.

Through my own personal experience and many prayer sessions spent with people dealing with this topic, the areas that seem to cause us the most pain and shame are: the use of pornography; masturbation that's become an addiction rather than healthy release; the breaking of personal sexual boundaries (particularly if celibacy has been chosen or seen as a spiritual imperative due to not being in a marital relationship); same-sex attraction (where an individual may not feel able to embrace an orientation due to their or other's beliefs, and also fear of rejection); and adultery.

In the next chapter we'll look at two areas mentioned above which are a real challenge for many across the board: pornography and masturbation. These two span across every category of person, key stage of life, sexual orientation, relational status, and culture. And boy, do we need some kindsight!

Before we turn our thoughts to this topic, however, there is another issue that ii coming more and more to the fore in the current age: that of body image.

Body image

Due to such high levels of objectified sexual imagery in films, advertising, pornography, and most aspects of our media, it is no wonder that we have a warped perception of the human body.

We have "mainstream" magazines for both men and women on the shelf next to *Country Living* and *AutoTrader* that worship a perfect body, perfect hair, and celebrate teeth that remind us of ceramic, glossy white tiles. We see a ripped six-pack as the elite for a man's torso, and we see 36GG breasts with pert nipples and flat stomach (all airbrushed) as the minimum standard for women's bodies.

So what do the rest of us do that don't sport these attributes? Or who don't look anything remotely like a sexualized Ken or Barbie? We believe the lie that we're either not good enough – or, even more pervasive and rarely discussed, we subconsciously pass on to our partner that they're not good enough because we've somehow accepted the world's sexual advertising as normal and therefore our partner isn't "sexy" enough in comparison. No wonder there are lots of very lonely people in the world. Because there are those who are now so "sexualized" in their thinking, they have no idea what it is to look at the actual person and make love to them and not some idealized person with 36-24-36 measurements or a six-pack.

Truly making love to someone includes seeing – and still celebrating – stretch marks, drooping testicles and hairy ears, blackheads on her back, spots on his bottom, sagging breasts, wobbly stomachs, and big toenails too hard for the average pair of scissors. This is the reality! This is the majority of men and women. So, is what we're saying that as a society we're not worthy of sexual expression unless we're young, nubile, pert, and pristine? Of course not, but it's sadly close to the false belief system our society operates with! Friends, we need a revolution in this area!

A wee sideline of a story. I know a kind, missionally minded Christian couple in their fifties. You know the sort. Salt of the earth. Pillars of the local community and church. Godly, inspiring, and prophetic, this couple do everything together. They have a wonderful marriage and have been enjoying this marriage for well into thirty years. And I hope they don't read this book – they will probably know who they are but thankfully no one else will. Here it is – they are two of the most highly sexed people I know. I once went on holiday with them to the countryside, staying in a small cottage. The noises coming from their room were remarkable. They sounded like two mating ferrets in a sack, with the addition of whoops and delighted groans. It was a long night for me. On my own in a single bed with a crackling FM radio for company.

Once over the shock, however, I thought just how wonderful it was. That for them to be with someone for that long, for them to have journeyed some hard roads together, to have "lost" the physical botox of youth – and both because of all that and in looking past some of that, they were still making love like it was their first time.

Sex, sex everywhere, and not a drop to drink…

Sadly, many people have the opposite dilemma. No sex drive. There are a few umbrella clinical terms for low sexual interest. They are Hypoactive Sexual Desire Disorder (HSDD) or Inhibited Sexual Desire (ISD). Not all clinicians and researchers agree with the varying definitions under these two terms but it's fair to say the overarching diagnosis is the same. That is, according to the *Psychology Today* website: "a low level of sexual interest resulting in a failure to initiate or respond to sexual intimacy."[21]

This affects both male and female alike, although it is more common in women. ISD affects one in five people. There may be varying determinants across the two genders as to causation, but most often it will be related to a combination of issues such as:

- low self-esteem

- poor body image

- negative sexual experiences, including abuse

- unresolved trauma

21   https://www.psychologytoday.com/conditions/sexual-desire-disorder.

- inability to form meaningful relationships

- performance-related anxiety

- medical reasons, such as low testosterone, depression, or as a side-effect of taking anti-depressants

- lifestyle choices that have a physiological effect, such as smoking, drinking in excess, or taking recreational drugs

- being overweight and or non-active

- stress

- relationship difficulties, such as conflict or rejection.

Sexual apathy in a relationship is very painful. Not just for the person struggling with the "loss" of something they may have once found joy-filled (or indeed, they may in fact never have experienced desire), but also, it may be emotionally painful for the partner (perhaps predominantly so). It takes a strong relationship to be able to weather situational or general sexual inhibition; both parties must be prepared to talk at all costs, and regularly, to get through this!

Sex forms part of our relational glue, and in the most appropriate way, if in a committed and monogamous relationship – it ties two souls together, as we'll discuss later in this chapter. It creates a deep bond. A God-ordained exclusivity between two people is precious. Without this glue, it's incredibly easy to become detached from the other partner. If one party refuses to talk, face the situation, or make genuine effort to show physical, if not sexual touch, while the apathy is present – then there's a recipe for disaster ahead.

Conflict and contempt within the relationship can often be cited as the reason why sex is withheld. There's a parody of the frustrated, tired, grumpy wife, who is sick of her husband and so avoids sex at all costs, both out of contempt for him and to punish him. Headache after headache, she rolls over on her side when any intimate advances are made by him as a sort of "protest" at how inept he is.

What may surprise us is how many wives share with me that the same is also true of their husbands. When I dig a little deeper, it is intriguing. In general, the women who are shunned sexually by their partners are all capable women; having partnered not because they *needed* a mate, but because they *wanted* a mate – there's a huge difference. A number of women have shared that they have been accused of "causing" the issue by not being attentive enough to their partner, with one sharing that she was told she was too "independent" and that as a result he had withdrawn sexually. The women I have spoken to have also shared that their respective roles within the marriage are confusing and they don't feel able to operate to their full potential.

The men I've spoken to have expressed that "she's always 'at me'"; "she's never happy"; "she's gained too much weight"; "she's too focused on the children"; "she's trying to be too controlling". I wonder what the real issue might be here. There's certainly something around a "competition" of the "sexes". Neither party feels fulfilled and secure. The male isn't celebrated or understood and therefore the female is rejected and becomes more bitter, which in turn amplifies her negative behaviours. The female isn't celebrated or understood and therefore the male is rejected and becomes more withdrawn, which in turn amplifies his negative behaviours. Everyone is losing out. Any couple facing these dilemmas has but one option if there is any chance of the relationship to be redeemed: to deeply and meaningfully communicate about what's really going on. And to choose to be accountable and honest, however hard the situation gets. Seek prayerful guidance, find a competent marriage counsellor, share with trusted friends – a lot of support is needed.

Regardless of the gender of the one withholding, or the reason (perhaps even conflict or contempt), sexual apathy cannot become concretized in a relationship. It's not fair on the other party to keep them in an enforced celibacy. It's not biblical, it's not kind, and it's not respectful of each other's physical needs. In fact Scripture references this in 1 Corinthians 7:5a: "Do not refuse and deprive and defraud each other [of your due marital rights], except perhaps by mutual consent for a time, so that you may devote yourselves unhindered to prayer" (AMP). The King James Version also uses the term "defraud". A strong word! It is from the French "to cheat someone from". To withhold a sexual intimacy in marriage is to cheat our partner from something beautiful and unique, precious and bonding.

There's no fudging this one. There's no way round our responsibility to each other. Even if we are miffed or angry, we have a responsibility to sort out our hearts and minds in order to be receptacles of love and forgiveness – to both give and receive of these virtues. "I just have a mental blockage when it comes to sex, I can't help it" – sorry, not good enough; "I'm just not interested, it'll change eventually" – sorry not good enough; "he/she should stop bothering me about it, and just be happy with who I am" – sorry, certainly not good enough. When we embark on a lifelong commitment with someone we give up our rights to withhold our body from our partner. The two verses preceding the one quoted above read:

> *The husband should give to his wife her conjugal rights… and likewise the wife to her husband. For the wife does not have authority over her own body, but the husband does. Likewise the husband does not have authority over his own body, but the wife does.*[22]

Mutual ownership of each other's bodies, full stop. Not sole ownership of our own bodies. As Song of Songs states: "My beloved is mine, and I am his."

If I had a penny for every time I've had someone say to me, "But I just don't feel like it; surely I shouldn't have to if I don't feel like it". Sounds right, doesn't it? It fits in with our culture of self. But the Kingdom way is to give out of the little we may have, rather than give a lot when we have plenty. This is explored in the Gospels with the widow who gave an offering at the Temple of two very small coins – all she had to live on.[23]

22 1 Corinthians 7:3–4, ESV.
23 Mark 12:41–44.

You could argue that this is equally as relevant for our emotions, finance, and yes, sex.

(Of course, there are certain scenarios where ownership is not considered mutual; where minds becomes warped and one's thoughts and actions may imply to the other "your body isn't your yours, it's mine". As in any partnership, there must be an element of give, and an element of take; serving each other according to covenant principles, but there is no room for emotional or sexual manipulation in mutual, respectful relationships.)

I can recall having multiple conversations with both men and women who have been incredibly hurt by their partner's sexual disinterest. It has the capacity to eat away at the self-esteem of people, not to mention laying wide open temptations and other available routes for sexual fulfilment that are not being provided for in the marriage. The very place where it should be cherished, have free rein, and be used for the glory of God and delight for each other.

Perhaps another way of viewing it is this. Every week or so we need to fill the car with petrol. The rain is lashing down, and the sky is grey. The bank account is low and a full tank is very expensive. There's a pressing need to fix the boiler, to buy the groceries, and to pay the gas bill. And we're shattered. And *X Factor* has just started. But… We have to go to work on Monday in the car, after taking the kids to school, after dropping off the missus in town for her hair appointment. So, there is no choice but to get out in the cold and rain and fill up the tank. To not do so would be to jeopardize our work, our kids' school, and the missus' perm. So we do it. We count it as part of our life responsibility. We own it even when it costs. And we're certainly not reliant on it being a euphoric moment in our life. When sexual apathy hits our lives – so it is the same as filling the car with petrol. It's a necessary thing to do, to keep everything healthy and safe, secure and functioning. Even if, at times, it's not on our top 100 list of most fulfilling moments. There will, God-willing, of course be times when fireworks erupt. Hold on to those moments. Let's hope they are regular occurrences. But when it's not… Fill the car up with petrol.

I can hear some men saying, "I hear you, Tarn, but what if I can't *actually* fill the car up with petrol. Ahem. I mean… I can't perform. Erectile dysfunction. Mental blockage. The sun won't rise!" Or women panicking saying, for example, "I just feel numb, I know I won't orgasm, and it just makes me feel like I'm constantly letting him down." Let me share a story.

I once knew a terrific lady in her fifties. She was diagnosed with cancer and fought hard for her life for eighteen months. She went from a healthy size fourteen with a rouged, plump face to a size eight and became emaciated. Understandably, in the last few months of her life, her self-esteem in regard to her body was very low, as she felt unsexy and tired. Morphine patches covered her arm and a thin but noticeable down of facial hair had appeared due to the high dose of steroids she was on. Her throat and mouth were often ulcerated and her hair never did what she wanted it to after the subsequent loss and re-growth post chemotherapy. She had been married for over thirty years. She and her husband were utterly devastated at the situation, the loss of their retirement years together, the loss of planning the next holiday, the imminent ultimate loss of "them".

I had one of the most beautiful conversations with her in this time about her love life – initiated by her, I would hasten to add! That conversation has never left me, and I refer to it often. She shared that, regardless of how she felt about her body and however tired she was, she still wanted to do all she could to give her husband some sexual attention. She explained they had had their ups and downs in this area as her husband had suffered some stress-related illnesses over the years, but they never gave up. For her, sexual intercourse was now tricky, as she was in much general discomfort. However, she was still able to, in her words "use my hands and kiss". And they found a way to enjoy some sexually connecting time together. Even in her discomfort and even though it would have been perfectly understandable for her to refrain from sexual activity, she still gave selflessly. She "filled the car with petrol". Touch, intimate and meaningful, is more sensual and bonding than the act of sex when it is simply functional and emotionally disconnected. As this couple knew, to their advantage.

And what a stunning example of selfless love this is. With a little creativity and a desire to make something work, huge bridges can be crossed between two people, even if it's not the most perfect of scenarios. This husband and wife didn't shut down on each other; instead, in the depths of an imperfect situation, they found a way to express love against all odds. I wonder whether our "blockages" or "I just don't want to"s would lessen if we were to have the same approach? Perhaps ask, "What is it my partner needs?", rather than "Do I feel like it?"

Sex – a spiritual encounter

I was speaking at a men's conference a few years back. A well-known worship leader and his band were chilling in the back of the venue. One of the band, a warm and charismatic man, struck up conversation with me about my talk. It will be of no surprise to you to hear that my talk had been on relationships and sex. He began sharing with me his "take" on worship and sex. Not your average conversation, but as I say, people share the most remarkable things with me; it's a privilege.

I stood, and listened, in awe. He explained, "The coming together of two people, in love, making love, creating such enjoyment through and for each other is sheer worship. At moments in the love-making my wife and I stop and express our thanks to the Lord, for this gift, as our spirits are joined, and we enjoy the moment of worship."

Now! I have to say, that was a first for me: someone telling me that they worship through sex!

I've since asked a few friends whether they've been intentional about making love as an act of worship. On both occasions I was met with silence. And then a guffaw of embarrassed laughter. Then a red face. To which I replied, "You neither, then!"

What it showed me was how profound love-making could be, and also how little I had really experienced this type of relational and sexual depth. Whether in worship or not, what is startlingly clear is that sex is as much a spiritual encounter as a physical one. There's power in sex to not just touch our flesh but to touch our spirits and soul. Which further explains why shame is felt so deeply when sex is used in a way God didn't intend. Because it's not just our bodies that are affected, but our very self.

This powerful connection, as we have seen previously, has been given the name "soul-tie". Now this isn't a biblical word, in the same way that the word "Trinity" isn't found within the pages of Scripture, but it serves its purpose by explaining the concept which we can see woven in and through the Bible.

Teaching notes from Christian Restoration (CRi) give a few helpful analogies in introducing what a soul-tie is:

> *You could wrap a knife and fork up together in a napkin for years and they would never interact or bond with one another. They are not designed to.*
>
> *You could set a chair upon a floor for years and the two items would never interact or bond with one another. They are not designed to.*
>
> *We however, are different.*
>
> *As spiritual beings with a soul, living in a body, we are designed to interact and bond with our maker and with one another.*

Indeed God has created us for fellowship in such a deep and wonderful way that scripture describes us as being capable of being knit together.[24]

This knitting together is a soul-tie. And there are many variations. Here's a few pulled from Scripture:

- A group of people with a common goal: "So all the men of Israel were gathered against the city, knit together as one man." (Judges 20:11, KJV)

- Best friends: "And it came to pass, when he had made an end of speaking unto Saul, that the soul of Jonathan was knit with the soul of David, and Jonathan loved him as his own soul." (1 Samuel 18:1, KJV)

- Reliant on someone when needing help: "And David went out to meet them, and answered and said unto them, If ye be come peaceably unto me to help me, mine heart shall be knit unto you" (1 Chronicles 12:17, KJV)

- Relationship with other Christians: "that their hearts might be comforted, being knit together in love". (Colossians 2:2, KJV)

This knitting together can be a healthy, normal and companionship full of blessing: "I am a companion [knit together] of all that fear thee" (Psalm 119:63), or a destructive

24   CRi Teaching notes, "Understanding 'soul-ties'" (http://www.christian-restoration.com/soul%20ties.htm).

and unhealthy companionship that draws the worst out of us: "the same is the companion [knit together] of a destroyer" (Proverbs 28:24, KJV).

By God's design, however, sexual intimacy is the greatest of knitting needles. It is the most explicit of unions, so much so that in the books of Genesis, Matthew, Corinthians, and Mark, the phrase is used "so they are no longer two but one flesh".[25] That's one big knitted jumper! Where one person's wool is deeply intertwined with another's. True and pure intimacy. We bind ourselves to people's spirits and souls through sexual activity and, in the right relationship, this is an awesome God-intended thing.

The opposite of course is counterfeit intimacy. Where we're trying to experience the fullness of a sexual encounter but without the God-intended construct of togetherness and commitment. This could be by way of giving the gift of our sexual self away in the wrong relationship, even a one-night stand; a fleeting encounter; a long-term affair; use of pornography – these are all forms of counterfeit intimacy. And in all these areas a joining still happens but then a severing, which is never what was intended.

There's much to consider in this chapter. Might I invite us to reflect on some of the contents. I appreciate this is a tough topic and many will be feeling mildly awkward if not downright upset. Let's tackle this with kindsight. First and foremost, we are not to beat ourselves up, but instead with kindness toward

25   See Genesis 2:24; Matthew 19:6; 1 Corinthians 6:16; Mark 10:8.

our self, give ourselves permission to learn.

And with that attitude, think through our response to:

- taking seriously any areas of sexual shame where we need to forgive ourselves.

- addressing sexual activity we've engaged in that goes against our spiritual ethics and needs honesty, admission, and repentance.

- assessing how we see our bodies. Do we view them with acceptance or dislike? Do we need to realign our mental imagery so that we see beauty and glory instead of ugliness?

- being truthful as to how we see other's bodies. Have we become too sexualized in our thinking and have forgotten what's real and what's false about the world's sexual marketing campaign? Might we need to intentionally revisit our partner's body and make mental and spiritual choices to see it as glorious?

- facing the issue head on if we've withdrawn the gift of sex from our partner. Asking for forgiveness is a simple place to start. And begin to talk, however uncomfortable. Even just a hug, or stroking their hair, or a kiss on the cheek can start to move things gently back into an intimate arena.

- asking God to disconnect us from any negative soul-ties due to sexual activity that was counterfeit intimacy.

May the God of second chances restore each and every one of us. May our hearts be saturated with goodness, kindness, and self-control. May we see our fellow sojourners through the eyes of Christ, and may we guard and treasure the gift of sex, whatever stage of life we find ourselves in. Amen.

7

On Porn and Masturbation

Over the last few years, there has been a significant shift in the way that porn is accessed by its audience. With the anonymity that the Internet brings, porn can now be viewed by an ever-increasing audience who no longer have to pay for the privilege. With access available night and day, we now find ourselves living in a ubiquitous porn culture. Some of the statistics of recent reports are eye-watering.

Porn and masturbation – harmless, surely?

Here are just a few of the remarkable figures that have been recently gathered regarding porn usage:

- 34 per cent of female readers of the online newsletter *Today's Christian Woman* admitted to intentionally accessing Internet porn in a recent poll.[26]

- In March of 2002 Rick Warren's (author of *The Purpose Driven Life*) Pastors.com website conducted a survey on porn use of 1,351 pastors: 54 per cent of the pastors had viewed Internet pornography within the

26 "Statistics and information on pornography in the USA", http://www.blazinggrace.org/porn-statistics/.

last year, and 30 per cent of these had visited within the last thirty days.[27]

- According to a Focus on the Family poll, 1 October 2003, 47 per cent of US families said pornography is a problem in their home.[28]

- In 2015 it was reported that in the UK, over 41 per cent of men in church said they are addicted to porn, and that 1/5 of Christian women are using porn on a regular or semi-regular basis.[29]

What an epidemic! And these figures are only likely to have increased in the last decade.

What on earth is going on? Have you noticed how we've relegated the body to a "product" separate to that of the physical manifestation of the person inhabiting it? I sense this is the crux of the sexual dysfunction we have in our society today. This separation is staggeringly dangerous to our psychological health and well-being – socially, spiritually, and emotionally. It does not make for God-inspired, honouring, as-intended sex; nor does it aid constructive celibacy.

The separation of body and soul into simply a product that we have so embraced, is why pornography, or porn-sex, has become so normal, so palatable, and therefore so misused. Because we've collectively and possibly personally,

27   Ibid.
28   Ibid.
29   http://www.theway.co.uk/news-9821-over-41-of-men-in-church-are-addicted-to-porn.

allowed ourselves to separate someone else's body from their personhood. We do it from a distance. We can detach on multiple levels. We can amuse ourselves sexually without any commitment to an actual person. Once done, we simply close the mag, or shut the laptop, or switch our "stored porn-memory" off and move on to washing the car, taking out the bins, getting the school uniforms ready. The pornographic image we've just entwined with won't fart under the duvet and try and then hold your head under, nor annoyingly light up a post-coital cigarette, nor expect us to engage in their "love-language", nor challenge why we bought *another* pair of shoes or techno-gadget we'll never wear or use.

I've had to ask myself hard questions as to my attitudes and sheer lack of shock these days at our sexualized culture. I've also asked hard questions to the menfolk in my life – with varying degrees of enlightenment. And the female folk too, who are brave enough to talk about it with me. "Do you use porn?" I've asked, over a frothy double shot cappuccino, multi-tasking while wiping Weetabix off the baby, smiling encouragingly at the friend in question to "spill the beans". I appreciate it isn't the most British of questions. Although I've asked it. Many times.

And the answers to questions about others' use of porn always fascinate me. For men, but not exclusively, it tends to be focused on "release", feeling in-control, feeling potent and competent, detachment of the daily grind, including a fleeting exit from relationships that need "emotional investment" and/or are sexually unfulfilling. For women, but again, not exclusively, it tends to be about transporting themselves to a place where they feel sexy and adored, something too few women purport to feel in their "normal relationships".

Whatever the gender, and whatever the rationale, it is most often reported as being a mechanism for stress management. This is possibly because the neurochemicals released during sex and orgasm reduce stress, aid sleep, and, even if momentarily, bring peace. Which is why it is so addictive too.

I had a conversation with a friend recently (their gender shall remain neutral to aid anonymity) who shared that they had fallen into an addictive cycle of coming home from work, jumping in the shower, drying off, then turning on the PC in the study, and masturbating to a variety of porn sites. It was only after the orgasm/release/shedding the stress of the day, that they then got on with the evening: cooking, pouring a glass of wine, getting ready for Bible study group or the gym, and so on. No longer can they just go home, get changed, and start the night without masturbating, facilitated by porn.

Take a moment, and with kindsight I invite you, without beating yourself up, to review your attitude to porn. If it's a problem for you and you're caught in an addictive cycle, keep on reading: there's some support in the following pages.

Or are you an occasional consumer, get wracked with guilt, leave the scene for a few months, only to dabble in something when an urge comes? How might you feel if you could master the urge and stay porn-free altogether?

If you're tempted, but porn-free, you hold the hope for thousands wanting that freedom too. Keep on running the race!

Or if this entire chapter is making you wonder what planet you're living on and you have no idea what on earth possesses people, bless you.

Women and porn

It's really important at this stage to blow the myth that porn and masturbation is a man's world. At one time, perhaps, but there's more and more research being published about women's growing addiction to, and use of, pornography. The previous statistic shows that 34 per cent of women who read a Christian online resource use pornography. There is little to suggest this figure increases or decreases whether of a faith persuasion, but a 2013 Ann Summers survey showed that 40 per cent of women accessed pornography at least weekly.[30]

Nichi Hodgson wrote in *The Telegraph* newspaper in August 2014:

> *Women are just as capable of being "addicted" to*
> *porn as men. It's official. A new German sex study has*
> *confirmed what I have long suspected and that heavy use*
> *of pornography could make some of us "hypersexual" –*
> *a personality disorder that involves spending excessive*
> *time engaged in sexual fantasies. We love a dopamine*
> *hit as much as the next fella. After all, we're human,*
> *and our brains are wired to find novelty exciting,*

30   As reported in *The Daily Mail*, 15 November 2013 (http://www.dailymail.co.uk/femail/article-2507752/Over-half-women-regularly-watch-porn-daring-40-admit-making-own.html).

*irrespective of our genitals or gender. I love porn, and
ever since I began researching it for my work, I've become
increasingly seduced by its gushing celebration of the
human body in all its variety; its capacity for pleasure
beyond the bounds of moral, missionary stricture; and
the fantasy outlet it provides. Far from believing that
porn is responsible for our social and intimate decay, I
am zealous about its capacity to cheer up our stress-rich,
time-poor, care-worn lives. Whatever the fantasy you'd
like to explore, there's a porn clip out there for you. If
you're female, you might just need to spend a little more
time riffling through the racks, so to speak.*[31]

Oh my days… I felt like yelling at her. OK, I did yell at her, or rather the article, at the breakfast table, paper in hand. I felt furious. Because I deal with the aftermath, no, in fact, the during-math and after-math. Men, and more and more women, addicted, scared, lost, and lonelier than they ever imagined they could be because of a sexual addiction they are now trapped by. And there are not enough pastors/leaders/ Christian sex therapists out there who are trained, equipped, insightful, unfazed, and non-judgmental enough to deal with this epidemic. (Though the ones I know of are superb.)

A while back, when ministering to a group of Christian women on sex and sexuality, a youngish attractive lady in

31   Nichi Hodgson, "The intimate confessions of a female porn fan", 7 August 2014 (http://www.telegraph.co.uk/women/sex/11019232/Porn-Why-us-women-love-watching-sex-play-out-online.html).

her mid-thirties asked to talk to me separately. We went and found a quiet corner, whereupon she wept and wept. Uncontrollably. Once she was able to talk, she shared that she was racked with a pornographic addiction. As a single lady, living on her own, she was succumbing to hours and hours a week of both webcam involvement and when not live streaming, was creating fantasy roles in her head accompanied by masturbation. Her fantasies were certainly *not* that of the Mills and Boon ilk, that is, woman falls into arms of strong man who then "takes" her, in the missionary position of course, whereupon she climaxes loudly after just but a few thrusts. Not that that's most people's version of normal either – thankfully! (Don't write in, friends, with your stories!) You get the gist.

Instead, her fantasies had become dark, merciless, and confused. Not for putting on paper. Some of you will be surprised at this. A woman. A Christian woman. Trapped in sexual perversion and addiction. Don't be shocked. With the influx over the last decade particularly of internet sex: chatrooms, sex forums, swapping sites, dogging sites – all as accessible as ordering an online food takeaway or viewing a show on catch-up TV we've missed – men and women, of faith and of none, are getting into all sorts of painful, shame-inducing sexual predicaments.

Men and porn

The Reverend Carl Beech, my dear friend, my children's godfather and co-minister in all things taboo, has worked tirelessly in this arena to support men who have found themselves caught up in a lifestyle of pornography.

I asked him to pen some wisdom for us. He writes:

We live in a massively visual age. Branding and image is everything and companies work very hard indeed to catch our eye. In fact, their methods have become increasingly sophisticated and specific. A classic example would be Diet Coke vs. Coke Zero. They both use the same artificial sweetener, are made by the same company and are bottled in the same manufacturing plants. They claim to taste slightly differently (I can't really tell the difference, if I'm honest) but apparently it's got a more sugary full-fat taste. But the significant difference is in the labeling. There's more to a label than you might think.

Researchers soon realized that a major percentage of the drink-buying general public weren't buying diet drinks… the men. Diet drinks were being associated with women. Men? Well they just buy the full-fat version because it is more manly to shove loads of sugar down your neck. And so the advertising copy boys came up with a label and brand specifically targeted at young men. It worked. The marketing never really mentioned the more full-fat taste; it focussed on the image. 55 per cent of Coke Zero buyers are men and by all accounts, a whole new group of men at that.

The porn merchants know how to catch our eyes too. Make no mistake, they know what buttons to press and when to press them. And it works. It is estimated that the industry is worth a staggering $97 billion a year (globally).[32] Someone somewhere is driving around in a red Ferrari off the back of blokes everywhere feeling like their lives are being dragged into the gutter by the whole thing. I'm not just giving you rhetoric. Over many years of mentoring men I've seen depression, marriage breakdown, loss of faith, suicidal thoughts, loss of libido, shame, guilt, their being caught by their kids looking at stuff, and more.

I guess one of the many problems with porn is that it's most often used in secret. Its usage takes place in the hidden places and in the dark. You create a compartment in your mind that no one else has access to and like a cancer it slowly eats at you until eventually it breaks out of the compartment and kills you emotionally. Often taking others with you.

So what do we do?

Some would take a brutal approach and say, "Well, just grow up and stop looking at it…"

Easier said than done for many people though. What we often don't talk about is that pornography isn't the only issue: it's the fact that you masturbate while looking at it, but

32   As stated on http://www.nbcnews.com/business/business-news/porn-industry-feeling-upbeat-about-2014-n9076.

143

no one really talks about that. I've noted over the years that often guys getting hooked on porn are actually hooked on the endorphin release that having an orgasm gives you. However, like all addictions there's a sting in the tail. The problem is that because the deed is done in the hidden and secret places, within seconds of "finishing" you just feel down and depressed. A moment of pleasure for hours of feeling pretty crap. Some guys get hooked on golf, others might go running, some are hooked on work. We all have our ways of medicating but this is pretty toxic and tends to run alongside all the other stuff.

So, how can we tackle this? Here's a way forward in the form of a list of bullet points (we men love a good list, right?):

- *Are you in a group of mates that you can share really openly with in an informal setting, maybe over a curry, and just share how you are doing in life, sex, work, health, etc.? It'll change the game if you do that.*

- *If you've prayed for forgiveness, remember to forgive yourself as well. Seriously. Too many men are trapped in guilt. Give yourself a break.*

- *Are you stressed out? Are you trying to medicate? Start to be kind to yourself and give yourself some space.*

- *If you are married commit to focus all of your head space sexually to your wife.*

- *Make a covenant with your eyes and train your eyes not to wander and undress women.*

• *Don't beat yourself up if you fail.*

• *Try praying and fasting. It's more powerful than you think.*

• *Focus on Jesus and not the porn problem. If I say "Don't think about pink elephants!" what's now in your head? So don't keep talking to God about your love of porn. Start to tell him good things, worship him, and pray for others. It'll divert your attention.*

• *It's this guy's opinion that all porn is wrong but that not all masturbation is. It's what's in your head that's the issue and why.*

• *Perhaps try remembering that every woman represented in a porn film or image is potentially your sister in Christ… that changes the way you see her. No longer an object for your own satisfaction.*

• *Note the law of diminishing returns. So often, after a short period of time, men find that ordinary porn no longer satisfies and it starts to take you to places you don't want to go and never even thought about. Be warned.*

Did I mention to forgive yourself and give yourself a break?

Revd Carl Beech, Director of Church Development and Church Development, Elim and Christian Vision for Men (CVM)

Masturbation

I've often been asked the question Carl Beech raises above, as to whether masturbation itself is an issue, never mind accompanying it with pornography! It's a widely debated topic. And it's fair to say that the argument will be different for those of faith, those of some, and those of none! Simply because the Christian's approach to sex will be informed by God's moral agenda, as opposed to a humanistic agenda.

With kindsight over the years, I've established a few parameters to bear in mind and to help on this issue. We all have to work out what feels right before God, and for ourselves. Albeit I'm with Carl on this, I don't feel all masturbation is wrong: it's what's in thoughts and the motivation that matter.

There is a framework I use when discussing this with people. It starts with the primary, over-arching question "Does what I do in a solo capacity sexually, support and nurture my spiritual, psychological, and relational health?" In order to answer this, we need to ask some tough questions, and answer them honestly! Are you ready?

1. If you're in a covenant relationship with someone, do you declare your solo-sexual activity to them?

- If yes, and there are agreed parameters and accountability, this is really healthy.

- If no, would what you're doing alone sexually feel acceptable to them? Or would it feel like a betrayal?

2. Are you free of shame while masturbating or afterwards?

3. Could you invite Jesus into your mind at the same time as masturbating and it still feel congruent? (This for some people is a proposal worthy of a mammoth internal cringe – perhaps not even because of any appropriate guilt, but the fact that as a society we've disassociated God from anything sexual, even the thought that the two could occupy the same space feels remarkably uncomfortable. Unpacking that is worthy of another book entirely!)

4. Are you a more integrated individual due to your solo-sex life? (Feel more "whole", alive, alert, and in touch with God?)

- If there's more than one "no" to these four questions, I would suggest we're not at ease with what we're doing and need to gain some further perspective. If, however, we're responding with a "yes" – then we may we have reached a spiritual and personal agreement about our own sexual ethic.

I'm also loath to talk about masturbation in terms of it being the single person's dilemma. It's not. We may or may not be in a position to have our sexual urges fulfilled through the "Scriptural mandate" of husband and wife, and even for those who are married or in a civil partnership, this is certainly neither a guaranteed context for sexual unity nor fulfilment either. Therefore, the issue and ethics of masturbation, outside joint mutual masturbation within the relationship, is as much of an issue with married people as with single.

An article in *Today's Christian Woman* reads:

> *At a purely biological level, masturbation isn't that much different than other things we do with our bodies – like picking our noses. Toddlers do both. They are wired to touch their bodies everywhere and repeat touching where they find pleasure. Little boys and girls quickly discover that their "private parts" feel really good to touch. As children grow, wise parents gently teach that touching some places of our bodies isn't appropriate to do in public. And they teach their kids not to pick their noses in public either.*
>
> *But why does picking your nose have an embarrassing but non-moral stigma, while masturbation has become laden with tremendous guilt and shame? While there is nothing inherently wrong with touching yourself to experience pleasure, masturbation becomes a moral issue because it involves sexuality. Sexuality has intrinsic moral implications. Does that mean that masturbation is always immoral? I don't think so.*[33]

For those of faith who are trying to "honour God with their body" (1 Corinthians 6:19–20),[34] the issue isn't about the

---

33 Dr Juli Slattery, "Masturbation: Is it Wrong?", *Today's Christian Woman*, May 2014 (http://www.todayschristianwoman.com/articles/2014/may/masturbation-is-it-always-sin.html).

34 The full text referred to here is: "Don't you realize that your body is the temple of the Holy Spirit, who lives in you and was given to you by God? You do not belong to yourself, for God bought you with a high price. So you must honour God with your body."

avoidance of pleasure. If it were, God would not have created thousands of nerve endings in the penis and perfectly designed the clitoris, which serves no other purpose than being a pleasure button! So if it's not about the avoidance of pleasure, can we honour God with our bodies and masturbate?

I think every person and every situation is different and there's no blanket answer for all. If someone has an addictive personality, experiences high levels of anxiety, and feels loneliness keenly, I would imagine developing a masturbation habit, probably accompanied by porn is **not** going to be a harmless, life-affirming use of time. However, if one masturbates using imagery in the mind that celebrates the beauty of the physical form instead of lusting after someone specific that isn't ours to ravage, nor uses porn – and if it helps manage our "urges" so that we can focus constructively on life, rather than being "consumed with passion" then that would seem to be a healthy, mature sexual approach.

There is a counter argument, however. In 1 Corinthians 7:9 we read, "But if they can't control themselves, they should go ahead and marry. It's better to marry than to burn with lust." Some would read this Scripture as a clear indication that any sexual expression is only permitted with another person, therefore, and should not be a solo endeavour. And not just with another person, but a *marriage* partner.

The case builds, some have argued, if we consider what Scripture might have said if solo-sex was permissible... surely it would have read something along the lines of, "But if they can't control themselves, they should go ahead and stimulate themselves in order to alleviate the tension. It's better to masturbate than to burn with lust." But it doesn't. It's clear on what it considers to be the planes' take-off strip: marriage. I'm personally not convinced that using the argument of what Scripture *might* have said is a sturdy one at all... although I understand how many people interpret 1 Corinthians 7:9 and how they choose to read into the text what *isn't* affirmed as much as what *is*.

Zero solo-sexual stimulation outside a marriage would seem then to perhaps be a possible "discipline". And for some people this would be a very positive life choice. It would certainly help those who may have temperaments better suited to abstinence rather than risking opening Pandora's box!

While at Bible college some years back now, I was fortunate to have both female and male close friends. I think the combination of both is a real gift, as I've had the privilege – through honest friendships – of learning candidly about the male psyche as well as the female, often more difficult to explore when in a romantic dalliance. One of my single male friends, with whom I enjoyed a fun-yet-meaningful platonic relationship, had looked deeply and carefully into this area of masturbation. At points in his life it had been a struggle for him. He was desperately wanting God to be the biggest influence in his life, and he intuitively knew that, for him, the continuance of a solo-sex life was playing havoc with his spiritual life. Through the process of stimulating himself, he was tapping back into all the previous sexual experiences he'd had, feeding off them, and was constantly re-opening the sexual memory banks that were still stored in his brain. And in his words, this left him feeling spiritually "foggy". Like there was shroud around him that meant he couldn't communicate as freely and as clearly with God as he'd like. So, he chose abstinence. I'm sure it wasn't always easy, but he flourished, as a man, in his gifts, and with God. That choice was right for him, and I often remember feeling very proud of him. He taught me a lot about sexual character and growth.

This story supports the somewhat more pragmatic argument that to masturbate is to enliven and arouse that which may be better served by being kept dormant. There's even a Scripture that some use in their theological reasoning to bolster this line of thought, although I consider this to be related to sexual intimacy with a partner as opposed to our current topic of self-stimulation. The Scripture to which I refer is Song of Songs and it reads in 2:7: "Daughters of Jerusalem, I charge you by the gazelles and by the does of the field: Do not arouse or awaken love until it so desires." I can intellectually understand that there's wisdom in not prematurely arousing something (although I don't understand being charged by a gazelle or doe!). Nonetheless you could argue that *by masturbating* one is preventing the arousal or awakening of love with another. It may therefore allow for the urge to be managed in order that one doesn't rush into an incompatible marriage; or instigate intimacy outside of that long-term commitment.

And it still doesn't answer the question of whether masturbation's permissible, and indeed taking that one step further: whether masturbation is something to nurture and celebrate.

What is clear, even from trying to write this chapter, is that there's much ambiguity on this topic, from Christian opinion through to Scripture. This is difficult, as there is so much room for varying degrees of interpretation, which in turn means there's more than one approach to truth. Our interpretation will be informed by our world view, our experiences, and the stream of faith in which we flow.

But with kindsight, by not beating ourselves up, but instead choosing to learn, we can only live and act with personal integrity. There's not a lot else that matters if we have that and can stand by it, before God and others.

8

On Finally, Choosing Comrades Well

In the last few chapters we've looked at romantic and sexual relationships, what it takes to ensure they're the best they can be, and how to look ahead if they're not what you might have hoped for. But these are of course just one sliver of the plethora of relationships we will encounter in our lives.

A combination of friends, relatives, and possibly a partner usually make up the largest chunk of adult-interaction in our lives. That said, the number of hours we work to make ends meet these days is astronomical and therefore time spent with co-workers is disproportionate in comparison with the time we spend with friends and family. There have been months on end, pre-children, when I've clocked up over sixty hours a week with colleagues and just six hours with family and friends! Not a good formula – unless your workmates are also great friends. Now that's a nifty combination! It's certainly worth putting in some serious effort with co-workers. Some of the greatest of friendships can be forged due to working together on a common purpose.

Friendships are one of the most life-affirming blessings. They're nourishment for the soul. But let's not kid ourselves: when they go wrong, they can also be an acute source of pain. My experience is that when friends let you down, it hurts deeply because, unlike family, there's been a conscious decision to share life with that person: we didn't have to, but we chose to. And typically we chose to share our foibles and weaknesses as well as our strengths. In other words, meaningful friendships invite us to be vulnerable together. When that vulnerability then gets run roughshod, betrayed, or discarded, it can feel like a fairly hefty rejection.

In the name of research I ran a poll through Facebook a few months ago and asked what the top three qualities are that people look for in a friendship. The responses came in fast, with people sharing their thoughts very candidly.

Loyalty, acceptance, and humour ranked at the top.

There were a further thirty-seven qualities offered, ranging from truthfulness to unconditional love; from quality time to generosity, with this most hilariously honest post winning the prize for the most outrageous: "Laughter, honesty and a love for life, shares in your good and bad times, oh and got to be fatter, older and uglier than me!!" (written by my former PA and chum – you can see why I love her!).

Loyalty, acceptance, and humour. A solid triune proposition. Let's look at their opposites, then. What we most dislike or fear in our friendships are: disloyalty, rejection, and humourlessness.

I just wonder how many of us have experienced, even in part, any of these negative characteristics in our friendships? Or, just as importantly, how many of us, if entirely honest with ourselves, have exhibited any of these negative traits? I have (in answer to both questions). Mitigating circumstances may hold firm in our minds, perhaps particularly to the latter question, but with honest kindsight, we grow in life, not by ignoring what's gone before, nor beating ourselves up for it, but learning from it. And I have chosen to learn both from what I've been very hurt by and ensuring I don't replicate them, but equally, to learn from what I have been embarrassed by in my behaviours, and without fail, ensured I don't repeat them.

Is there a moment of reflection you might take at this point, and think through where, with kindsight, you acknowledge both being hurt but also maybe hurting another? May I suggest that where we've been hurt, we forgive (because we too are forgiven according to the central principle of Christian theology), and then where we've hurt someone, we seek to offer our apologies? A card sent, an SMS pinged, a call made. Friendships are too precious to lose because of pride, stubbornness, or apathy. When all the cards are shuffled, and the deck is dealt, the value of the hand can be weighed largely by the friends and family we have.

Regardless of my friendship failings over the years, the successes seem to have outweighed the failures. Thankfully, oh so thankfully, as I type today I feel humbled by the vibrant, loyal, truthful, beautiful friendships I have in my life now, many of which are now decades long. They are just the best anyone could hope for.

But they don't just happen. Even if we think they do! We've already seen that certain qualities really matter. Years back, I had a conversation with a wise young curate, a top-notch friend, on the topic of friendships. I said, "I don't know what I've done to deserve the friends I have!" And he quipped back, "Well, you must have done something! It's probably that you chose well" – and blow me down, he was right; it really got me thinking. What I had done, whether I had realized it or not, was to become a little more discerning than I was in my twenties about the people I invested into and whom I invited to invest into me. Hence, I was building friendships on rock and not sand.

I recently sat and wrote a list of the people I would now call my closest friends. I worked out there were two "special buddies": the ones who know me sometimes more than I do myself – and fifteen close friends: the ones who know me fully, share life events and experiences with me, and who I know will still be around in fifty years' time. Then there were about thirty more people whom I would love to catch up with at a party, laugh raucously with, and share the latest. And on from that there were hundreds of jolly wonderful people I've met over the years with whom I stay in touch via social media and the like.

Among the special buddies and close friends, however, there was a common theme. They are all good, good people. They have morals and ethics. They have values about things that matter. They are committed to their families and friends and, interestingly, they really like themselves. They are loyal, they accept me wholeheartedly, and each in their own way are witty and funny. Are these friends perfect? No! Do they have foibles, tantrums, disagreeable tendencies, annoying habits, spinach in their teeth, fart accidentally when laughing too loud, make sweeping judgments, forget to text on anniversaries, and mess up every now and again? Yes! Phew! What a relief. All the things I do, then. I'm in good company. And so, it seems, they feel it's mutual.

Having reflected on Jesus' relationships, I realize He too had the same grouping of friends. He had three "special buddies": Peter, James, and John. The remaining nine disciples could be described as "close friends". Next come the 120 other disciples (faith community), and finally general interactions (wider network). Just as I did, let's take a quick stock check of our own relationships using that framework.

- **Special buddies**. Or family-of-choice as I like to call them. These are our inner circle and they are like gold dust. The best of our best investment goes into them.

- **Close friends**. These people bring depth and richness to our lives and give rhythm and a sense of belonging. They know us fully and us them, and quality contact ensures lives are entwined meaningfully into each other's.

- **Faith community and/or work/recreational community**. This group is made up of those in our church, place of work, or local community with whom we meaningfully interact.

- **Wider network**. This is the complex tapestry of people with whom our paths cross. Still meaningful, they may be friendships from a previous workplace, or college friends when we were younger who we see every few years, or those we will stay in touch with via social media.

This is a very useful framework within which to operate. It puts into context how many special buddies and close friends we can manage and sustain. If anyone could have had hundreds of special buddies it would have been the incarnate God – but rather even He chose to invest deeply into a small handful of people. I believe this is an excellent model for us to follow. Of course this isn't an exact science nor a biblical imperative to follow, but rather a tested approach.

This reflection and research led me to be able to summarize in three words that which I suspect helped me begin, all those years ago, to discern friendships a little more clearly: **chemistry, connection, and commonality**.

American pastor Bill Hybels used similar words when looking at whom he should employ in his church; in doing so he coined the phrase "character, competence, chemistry", which I've used as a regular recruitment tool too! But for the very different task of discerning friendships, I've found looking at chemistry, connection, and commonality is as good as it gets.

Chemistry

Chemistry between people is normally talked about in romantic terms: "There was such chemistry between us, we couldn't keep our hands off each other!" It's seen as being vital in order to make the relationship special and viable. If you've read Chapter 5, on falling in love, you'll know I have concerns with how much store we've placed on needing a "euphoric" high, romantically, at the cost of greater virtues.

However, chemistry is important, because it marks out a relationship as significant and, ultimately, enjoyable! It's no different in non-romantic relationships. It needs to bring something with "spark". So how, then, do we define chemistry in a friendship? What are the core components? A brief search on Google came up trumps. In response to the search terms "chemistry between people", up came an article on *Psychology Today* that, in relation to "chemistry between people", spoke of "non-judgmental, similarity, mystery, attraction, mutual trust, and effortless communication".[35] Quite a sassy little list there! I like it.

I might only swap one of those descriptive words, and that would be to have "spontaneity" instead of "mystery". Mystery sounds a little like "game-playing", as in: "I'll keep you in suspense in the friendship!" Not a good move. Spontaneity, however, suggests a willingness to engage in fun, to bring something out of the norm, and to keep things fresh. I adore people who do this in my life. When around them, they're like opening three sachets of space dust and downing them in one go – truly invigorating!

So chemistry is important. None of us want to be in personally costly relationships with friends who hold little personal attraction to us. (And if we do, then a counselling session is probably required, right there.) Does this sound harsh, or clinical almost? Am I running the risk of being exclusive in

35   Kelly Campbell, "Relationship Chemistry: Can Science Explain Instant Connections?", 20 August 2011 (https://www.psychologytoday.com/blog/more-chemistry/201108/relationship-chemistry-can-science-explain-instant-connections).

my assessment of friendships therefore? By placing the worth of a friendship on how good they make us feel? I don't think so. Because I think that would be to confuse, or confine, the varying types of friendship, connection, and commitment we can have with people. There are different levels of friendships. And that's OK. As we have seen, Jesus Himself, our role model extraordinaire, showed us these varying levels.

Connection

Of course, there will always be any number of general people we will rub shoulders with – unless we live in a vacuum devoid of others! We all have to negotiate work colleagues, neighbours, people at church, clubs, the gym, and friends of friends. Of course, depending on your outlook, you could see this as a rich opportunity to keep meeting new people and develop further friendships, or it could feel a bit overwhelming if we don't have good personal boundaries in place.

We need to give ourselves permission that we don't have to be special buddies with everyone we encounter, or even close friends with them. Unless there's obvious chemistry or a general well-being when together, then it's likely those people will stay part of our faith/work or recreational community or indeed wider network.

Sometimes, we just have to know our own boundaries and trust ourselves with them. If you struggle to identify where to put your time and effort, you could try asking yourself these questions, which I always find helpful when I'm working through potential new friendships.

- What space do I have to invest into another friendship? If I don't have the space, but feel the friendship is right to develop, how do I create the space? What might I need to review to do that?

- Will it detract me from friendships that I have already committed to? If so, how will I negotiate that?

- Is this person/couple/family meant to be in my life, and I in theirs for a reason, for a season, or for a lifetime?

The reason, season, lifetime concept isn't mine! It comes from a piece of writing by an unknown author. I've read and valued its advice many times over the years. It reads:

People come into your life for a reason, a season, or a lifetime. When you figure out which it is, you know exactly what to do. When someone is in your life for a REASON, it is usually to meet a need you have expressed outwardly or inwardly. They have come to assist you through a difficulty, to provide you with guidance and support, to aid you physically, emotionally, or spiritually. They may seem like a Godsend, and they are. They are there for the reason you need them to be.

Then, without any wrongdoing on your part or at an inconvenient time, this person will say or do something to bring the relationship to an end. Sometimes they die. Sometimes they walk away. Sometimes they act up or out and force you to take a stand. What we must realize is that our need has been met, our desire fulfilled; their work is done. The prayer you sent up has been answered and it is now time to move on. When people come into your life for a SEASON, it is because your turn has come to share, grow, or learn. They may bring you an experience of peace or make you laugh. They may teach you something you have never done. They usually give you an unbelievable amount of joy. Believe it! It is real! But only for a season. LIFETIME relationships teach you lifetime lessons; those things you must build upon in order to have a solid emotional foundation. Your job is to accept the lesson, love the person/people anyway and put what you have learned to use in all other relationships and areas of your life. It is said that love is blind but friendship is clairvoyant.[36]

I really like it, although of course there are limitations, not least that the "reason" they are in our lives could well be for us to serve them, as opposed to their just having concern for our well-being. I think it's helpful to think through friendships through this reason, season, lifetime lens, albeit as a helpful tool rather than a concrete way forward. Nothing in life is that easy to compartmentalize, least of all into a reason, season, or lifetime. Friendships are too special and beautiful to assign to time-bound labels. But the reason, season, lifetime concept is helpful as it provokes constructive thought as well as emotional enlightenment as to the positioning of the friendship in our life.

36   As cited on http://www.yuni.com/library/docs/631.html.

It may just be the permission we need not to have to take every friendship into a six-decade commitment!

Whether we're a raging extrovert who gathers friends like pins drawn to an enormous magnet, or a reflective introvert who carefully assesses the energy they have to expend on those around them – we all need friends. The challenge is to discern, particularly as years go by, how to maintain them and how to keep space open for new friends, and how to let go of some of them.

A friend of mine, who shall remain nameless, said to me once, "At the weekend the missus and I went through a list of all our friends to decide who we were going to simplify…" I stood, my mouth agape. He went onto explain, "With marriage; a growing family; church commitments; work-life balance; parents – the time we have for friendships is sadly slim, so we really need to make that time matter, with people who we feel it's right to give valuable time to and them us." Perhaps it was just the word "simplify" I reacted to, because once explained, I thought how eminently sensible he was being. Sincere, meaningful friendships are an investment. They take time to cultivate and time to keep them flourishing. And even if time available is short, then at least both parties need to be intentional about their friendship.

Some people have expressed that they feel friendships aren't to be chosen; they just happen to be those people who materialize in front of us. And if that's what people are most comfortable with, then ride that way, my friends! What I'm suggesting is that for those who want to be intentional as to whom they invest in, and who to allow to invest into them, when all around are time-pressured, it's OK, yes OK, to put a healthy framework around how we discern those friends.

So if we ascertain that it's not right for us to push into a new friendship, on whatever level, that's OK. It's really OK. It will take some honest and focused conversations, or at least some awareness as to how to manage expectations, but well worth it in the long term. Or of course, we could avoid the issue, open up our life to multiple people, struggle to have quality relationships with any number of them and burn out with carrying the load. Yes, I've done that too, and I know which I find more productive and beneficial!

Commonality

In 1960 C. S. Lewis wrote *The Four Loves*. In it,

> *he examines the differences between the four main categories of intimate human bonds – Affection, the most basic and expressive; Eros, the passionate and sometimes destructive desire of lovers; Charity, the highest and most unselfish spiritual connection; and Friendship, the rarest, least jealous, and most profound relation. In one of the most beautiful passages, he considers how friendship differs from the other three types of love by focusing on its central question: "Do you see the same truth[?]"*[37]

37   From Maria Popova, "C.S. Lewis on True Friendship" (http://www.brainpickings.org/2014/09/08/c-s-lewis-four-loves-friendship/).

"Do you see the same truth?" What a remarkable, simple, and profound idea: one worthy of a pause. Think over your friendships. Bring people's faces to mind. Consider the joyous or profound moments you've had together. Or even just the beautifully comfortable ones. I wonder whether these moments are there because you've instinctively seen the same truth allowing for a natural understanding between you? Or perhaps what's come to mind is a fractious friendship, uncomfortable perhaps because a natural understanding is missing?

I can see that with my friendships, particularly my special buddies and close friends, it's this space we inhabit. Natural understanding. Same truth. This same truth has glued us together even when other things have been really tough. It is of no surprise to me, therefore, that the majority of my friends have a deep Christian faith in a glorious and liberating God, as do I. This "same truth" largely informs our morals, ethics, and values, and of course, purpose in life.

But with that said, I've met many Christians, with the same truth, whom I would not be overly excited about having a close friendship with!

So, there it is: my tried and tested framework for healthy discernment for friendships. Chemistry, connection, and commonality.

Friendship – value to survival

C. S. Lewis also wrote,

> *I have no duty to be anyone's Friend and no man in the world has a duty to be mine. No claims, no shadow of necessity. Friendship is unnecessary, like philosophy, like art, like the universe itself… It has no survival value; rather it is one of those things which gave value to survival.*[38]

Boom! What a quote!

Friendship gives value to survival. Yes, that's it. That's really it. There have been five times in the past fifteen years when I have felt like I could have gone under. So on average, a tough stint every three years. Oh, my Father in Heaven, please could we get the average down, I'm begging!

During these notable painful episodes through my life (spanning relationship breakdown, bereavements, two miscarriages, working with challenging leadership, and everything in between) I wasn't sure how I would pull through the pain of some of these events, or their ensuing effects and consequences, nor whether I would be the same again. When all was stripped back, my faith, and then friendships, were really all I had left of any consequence.

When I just couldn't do it by myself, in the darkest of times, my closest friends gave me a plot, a plan, and reminded me of

38   *The Four Loves*, Harcourt Brace, 1960, p. 71.

my purpose. When I wondered if I'd survive emotionally, I'd look to them for a plot, which, at times, was as simple as "keep going". I'd look to them lost, imploring, and together we'd come up with a plan, which could be as endearingly practical as "Brush your teeth and get to work". And I'd listen to them as they retold me my story, my purpose – and reminded me of prophetic words spoken over my life, prayed for divine restoration, believed for me that I could hear the divine for myself, and modelled the beautiful heart of God in their reactions, responses, and faithfulness. They gave me a plot, a plan, and reminded me of my purpose. And I survived.

Henri Nouwen, one of my favourite spiritual writers, summarizes this in a different, but equally as honest, way. I've learned much from this piece of writing, and re-read it often.

> *When we honestly ask ourselves which person in our lives means the most to us, we often find that it is those who, instead of giving advice, solutions, or cures, have chosen rather to share our pain and touch our wounds with a warm and tender hand. The friend who can be silent with us in a moment of despair or confusion, who can stay with us in an hour of grief and bereavement, who can tolerate not knowing, not curing, not healing and face with us the reality of our powerlessness, that is a friend who cares.*[39]

39   Henri J. M. Nouwen, *Out of Solitude: Three Meditations on the Christian Life*, Ave Maria Press, 2004, p. 38.

Reassurance

One of my special buddies said once, "I will always stand with you, support you and love you, regardless". Priceless, precious, the most stunning words I could ever hear. My spirit and soul doubled in size, my shoulders went back, my face lifted. "I am not alone and I am loved," my soul sung. Such reassurance, kindness, and such loyalty. The reassurance that another would stand by me, loved me, and that I had no need to perform for any of this to be more true, was profound. I took her hand after her saying this, and said nothing, but I felt everything. I felt sure.

It reminded me of this Winnie the Pooh and Piglet moment:

> *Piglet sidled up to Pooh from behind.*
> *"Pooh!" he whispered.*
> *"Yes, Piglet?"*
> *"Nothing," said Piglet, taking Pooh's paw. "I just wanted to be sure of you."*[40]

It brings to mind Proverbs 17:17 ("A friend is always loyal, and a brother is born to help in time of need") and Ephesians 4:32 ("Instead, be kind to each other, tenderhearted, forgiving one another, just as God through Christ has forgiven you").

When loyalty is offered and when kindness is shown, the heart grows fuller. The friendship becomes safe, sure, worthy, symbiotic – in summary, interdependent. And these are the marks of a solid friendship. We are all in need of these types of friends.

40   A. A. Milne, *Winnie the Pooh*, Dutton Children's Books, 1996, p. 284.

We can't always choose our relatives...

Members of our family should be, after all, our friends as well. Some of us are delighted to say they are. But probably for many of us, at least one of our family relationship will be a bit of a struggle and can cause significant discomfort. Family relationships are a complex arena! Complex because it's harder to be objective about them, harder to "just walk away" because everyone and everything is so entwined, and harder to recover from a family relationship that goes wrong.

Oftentimes it's not that there's necessarily an explicit "issue" between family members, but rather just a lack of chemistry and commonality. We may get on fine with them, but it may be too high an expectation to consider they could enter the arena of a special buddy or close friend. Even if we've grown up with someone, had the same genetic identity, or the same life history, this doesn't mean there's going to be inherent understanding, kindness, reassurance, or "getting each other". Yet some of us may find that we still place a high expectation on our relatives to meet our emotional needs, live life out with us, enjoy who we are, and so on when, perhaps, they just can't. It does everyone a favour when some expectations are lessened and the relationship can reach its own natural balance.

I only have two immediate family members, excluding my children – my older sister and my dad, who has early-onset Alzheimer's. My mum sadly passed away from cancer in 2003. Of course, I have my wider family, all of whom get on well. It's fair to say my sister and I have to work hard at times to oil the cogs of our relationship. But respect for each other tries to plug the gap of "natural understanding".

I bumped into the sister-in-law of my sister at a conference the other day, and we had a lovely catch up, showing each other photos on our phones of our children. Another lady – who also happened to know my sister – joined in the conversation. She was evidently shocked that my sister and I were in fact sisters. My sister's sister-in-law began a mildly awkward, if not humorous, conversation explaining to the joiner-inner: "They're chalk and cheese. No, in fact, they're less similar than chalk and cheese." I chipped in with: "No, in fact, take that one step further! People have questioned whether we are in fact biologically related. Except that I look like my dad!" A slightly-too-long silence of awkward smiles followed! I cannot recall how many of these conversations I've had over the years. The fact that both my sister and I teach and preach, and are both in love with Jesus, is in itself remarkable for two sisters so totally different. But these really are the only similarities. We manage to remain on good terms because we care for each other due to our kinship.

However, there have been times over the years when I've felt sad that there's not a closer relationship with my sister. Disappointed, even. It's all about interpretation, isn't it, as I'm sure she too will have felt something of a disappointment in our relationship, at things I've not done, albeit that I've been unaware of it at the time, or in fact even today.

At times it's been easy to fall into the trap of romanticizing what it would have been like to have a big brother, for example, who would have protected me from some of the harm I came to; or to have a gaggle of sisters akin to those in *Little Women* who would have talked with me late into the night about boys and the best brand of sanitary towel. However! There's no accounting for what a brother would have actually been like: he may have been a narcissistic nightmare who ignored me morning, noon, and night! The same for a bunch of sisters – there's no evidence whatsoever to suggest there would be chemistry with them, however many there were! The reality is that we have what we have. The far healthier approach is to see the family we do have for what they are, rather than what they aren't, and with kindsight being honest (with self!) about any disappointments.

Most of us, when being kind and generous, can think of any number of attributes our family members have that are positive. Sometimes it just takes a bit of grace and humility to acknowledge them. It takes no humility for me to acknowledge how remarkable my sister is. She just is. And if and when those disappointments rise, kindsight prompts me to remember that my sister is a legend: wise and articulate, committed and faithful, and much more besides. It's a privilege to be her sister.

Take a kindsight moment to think about your family. Try to find one thing that you value about your close relatives, perhaps particularly the relatives with whom you've had a real struggle or even, as with me, just a sadness that there's not been more connection between you. If appropriate, make an opportunity this week to affirm them of what you do value: we can all think of one thing! Thank them. Let them know you are deeply grateful. Or you may be incredibly blessed with a close-knit family who just "get" you, and you them. They may really respect you, accept you, and love you. Then perhaps make this the day you give huge thanks for that. It's a rare thing, so celebrate!

I find I often applaud my friends but rarely affirm my family. This of course has its roots in what we perceive to be "choice". I've chosen my friends and they me. But my own family – I didn't choose them, nor they me. I cringe when I remember, all too clearly, yelling at my parents: "I didn't choose to be born", after yet another tantrum about what was probably a very reasonable request, such as being asked if I might tidy my room. But born I was. And I became a daughter, granddaughter, niece, and sister, choice or no choice. And very grateful I am too.

The choice we do have, whatever our circumstances, is how well we give of ourselves to our friends, relatives, and immediate family, even when we feel let down, hurt, or when we feel we've given more than they've returned. And we can model that choice to those around us, demonstrating what it is to be a great friend or family member with the hope that we become contagious! And discerning. And the setters of solid boundaries!

I pray that we each find friends and family who'll walk with us along the thousands of miles we'll walk in our lifetime. I pray that they will be people with whom we keep step: friendships full of the Holy Spirit, uplifted by chemistry, relished through connection and deepened through commonality.

To conclude, let me share one of my favourite poems.

And so one day
We fell in step.
It mattered not that each of us
Had traveled quite a way,
Or that the hour was rather late.
It just seemed very good
To walk together.

I think it seemed to each of us
A sweet surprise,
An unexpected joy
To know such deep and quiet peace
With one another.

Seemed strange that out of those
Who through the years
Had crossed our paths,
In this, life's richest afternoon,
We who had almost strangers been,
Were brought together.

Draw closer, friend,
And place your hand in mine.
And let me see about your eyes
That merry, crinkly smile
Which I have grown to prize.

L'envoi

It may grow late, it may grow very late.
I shall not see the shadows
Only stars,
If we keep step
Together.[41]

Sue C. Boynton

41   Sue C. Boynton, "We Walk Together", *Heart on My Sleeve*, Whatcom County Historical Society, 1980, as cited on https://thepoetrydepartment.wordpress.com/2010/10/08/we-walk-together/.

9

On the Incomprehensible: Stories of Injustice

Sometimes in life things happen that are simply incomprehensible. They make no sense and they leave us bewildered and afraid. Bewildered because they shouldn't happen, but they have. And afraid, because any security in what we anticipated life to be like is shattered. We're changed for ever. These days one glance of the news is enough to bear testimony to continual injustice. So much so that we may try to tune out and emotionally distance ourselves from what we're seeing – not as defiant disinterest, but arguably, as a necessary psychological approach to keep us sane and prevent compassion fatigue.

But sometimes, it's impossible to tune out, however hard we try! That's because either the injustice is happening to us. Or our loved ones. Or to those whom God has intended us to cross paths with, in order that we may be his hands and feet to those who are suffering. In 2012 I was introduced to an organization called Love146, an international NGO caring for children who'd been sexually and commercially exploited, globally. I was gripped with compassion for the children whom they were serving. I couldn't get my head around some of the stories of depravity: toddlers being traded like animals;

barely pubescent girls regularly found in brothels; young boys sleeping rough in European ports waiting for boats to come in, in order to sell their bodies to eager sailors and male tourists; children working eighteen-hour days in cannabis farms in some of the UK's finest counties.

I've been a supporter of the organization ever since and volunteer both my time and skills. Yet… it's one of the hardest things I've ever been involved with. Because I can't walk away. It's on my mind constantly. I can't tune out. To do so would be the *antithesis* of Micah 6:8 (NKJV):

> *He has shown you, O man, what is good; And what does*
> *the Lord require of you But to do justly, To love mercy,*
> *And to walk humbly with your God?*

My dreams are filled, at times, with imagery of exploited children, and in one particular dream, I see children that resemble my two little boys. I wake up distraught, disturbed, and sickened. I've more than once, when this has happened, gone to my boys' bedrooms and stroked their hair, praying protection and goodness over them with tears in my eyes. I'm the fortunate mother who can do that; many mothers globally have only empty cots or blankets to remind them of the child that's disappeared, or there are mothers who feel that there was no choice but to sell their child in order to prevent the rest of the family from starving. My boys are the fortunate ones – they have a mother to gently tiptoe into their room and pray over them – many children are alone, worked to the bone, "owned" by a devious trafficker, and never lovingly held by someone with a pure motive. The Lord requires of me that I do justice, love mercy, and walk humbly. This is a terrifically hard set of steps to take. But these are steps that have been walked before by many a good man and woman, and therefore it is possible. Eminently possible.

Love146 began with just a few of these Wilberforce-esque people. People who, themselves gripped with compassion, could not turn away any more. It's been a great pleasure of mine to work with the US co-founder Rob Morris, CEO Steve Martin, and their team. Rob writes of what spurned his "Micah" walk, on a visit to the Philippines.

> *We found ourselves standing shoulder to shoulder with predators in a small room, looking at little girls through a pane of glass. All of the girls wore red dresses with a number pinned to their dress for identification.*
>
> *They sat, blankly watching cartoons on TV. They were vacant, shells of what a child should be. There was no light in their eyes, no life left. Their light had been taken from them. These children… raped each night… seven, ten, fifteen times every night. They were so young. Thirteen, eleven… it was hard to tell. Sorrow covered their faces with nothingness.*
>
> *Except one girl. One girl who wouldn't watch the cartoons. Her number was 146. She was looking beyond the glass. She was staring out at us with a piercing gaze. There was still fight left in her eyes. There was still life left in this girl…*

All of these emotions begin to wreck you. Break you. It is agony. It is aching. It is grief. It is sorrow. The reaction is intuitive, instinctive. It is visceral. It releases a wailing cry inside of you. It elicits gut-level indignation. It is unbearable. I remember wanting to break through the glass. To take her away from that place. To scoop up as many of them as I could into my arms. To take all of them away. I wanted to break through the glass to tell her to keep fighting. To not give up. To tell her that we were coming for her…

Because we went in as part of an ongoing, undercover investigation on this particular brothel, we were unable to immediately respond. Evidence had to be collected in order to bring about a raid and eventually justice on those running the brothel. It is an immensely difficult problem when an immediate response cannot address an emergency. Some time later, there was a raid on this brothel and children were rescued. But the girl who wore #146 was no longer there. We do not know what happened to her, but we will never forget her. She changed the course of all of our lives.[42]

This type of work, with this type of organization, is not for the faint-hearted. I have had to engage with the philosophy of kindsight toward myself in many regards in order to emotionally stay afloat in this heart-wrenching environment. There are days when I feel as though I've blown it: when I feel as though I

42   As told on http://europe.love146.org/love-story/.

have not worked hard enough to make a difference; not been strategic enough with resources; not come up with enough ideas; not found enough money from enough philanthropists; not connected enough with those who could help. In general I've just not done enough. And then I stop, and breathe, and stop beating myself up, and look at it through kindsight.

What *will* help these children is if I use what I've learned since working on this battlefield, rather than be paralysed with false guilt and frustration as to what I'm not doing. That won't help anyone! I need to see myself as someone who's enrolled in the metaphorical school of Florence Nightingale, who's even prepared to be on the frontline, among bloody and broken bodies – and who may, on occasion, be able to save one life. To imagine that Florence could have saved every life, or even stopped the battle, is of course untrue. For her to ever have thought she could save every life and even stopped the battle would have been to have discarded her training, her knowledge, her purpose. And this lesson must be grappled with by many of us who work with the "incomprehensible".

It may be that we serve a life at a time; it may that we serve but one life in a lifetime. If you needed to hear that, I pray it will settle into your soul and bring you liberty – to do what you can, and re-focus from what you can't. I will be praying! Would you too pray for the work of Love146 and every agency trying to eradicate the injustice and horror that slavery in all its forms brings? Thank you.

It was my involvement in caring for vulnerable children that led to the inclusion of this next segment. And its inclusion is something I've prayed over more than any other area of the book. It's because it sits weightily with me simply due to its gravity. Yet it carries such potency given that we're now exploring incomprehensible injustice. When the idea for this book even came into being, one of the main precepts was that the book had to speak into situations that are oftentimes left unspoken about, even when it is hugely uncomfortable. We (me, my prayer support network, and a young friend of mine, about whom I'll speak shortly) prayed for the content of these pages to be meaningful to a majority audience, of faith or not, if not least to assist some people along the way, then to educate and inform. Truth, grit, honesty, imperfect things, harsh realities, painful events – they all had to be brought to the table and not be airbrushed on the pages to sanitize the reading experience. I've tried hard to do that this far and this segment is certainly no different.

So, we're now going to look at the true story of a twenty-seven-year-old friend of mine. She has modelled for me what it is to not just survive an incomprehensible injustice, but to work through it well enough so as to offer wisdom to others and remain determined to forgive. Unbelievable.

And so it is that I had the privilege a while back of speaking to a large audience at a well-known Christian conference. During the week I had shared at length about both my work with Love146 and anti-child-trafficking, and also my story of adopting two babies. The two stories, while not related, had some common themes, about God's love toward His most prized possession, his little children.

I told stories of how connected my heart is to my tiny sons, in that it feels set daily to burst with love and compassion toward them. I need no "working up of emotions" toward them; it's just there – in full measure. And if that's a human experience, I concluded, imagine how deep, connected, and pure that love and compassion is from our Father God, who through His Holy Spirit draws us to him in son-ship and daughter-ship.[43] And how God expects of us, those who enjoy this spiritual adoption, to showcase back to humanity the radical love of the Father to the widows and orphans: those with no human father to protect them. Hence my motivation and passion in protecting children from sexual and general exploitation. It's an expression of love due to my being loved.

A little later during the conference, a young lady in her twenties came to find me. She stood patiently, waiting for those around to thin out a little, and came to stand by the side of me. She asked to share something; I nodded encouragingly. Her words didn't come immediately. I held her gaze trying to ensure my eyes conveyed the patience and commitment I felt to listen to her, regardless of what was going on around us. She falteringly began to disclose her story. It was so brave of her. As her sentences began to flow I was flooded with compassion and love for her, while simultaneously feeling a rising anger at what she had gone through… She finished her story and I hugged

43   See Romans 8:14–16, "For all who are led by the Spirit of God are children of God. So you have not received a spirit that makes you fearful slaves. Instead, you received God's Spirit when he adopted you as his own children. Now we call him, 'Abba, Father'. For his Spirit joins with our spirit to affirm that we are God's children."

her. And there began a special connection. She taught me more about kindsight in five minutes than I had learned in a decade. In her words, she writes her story for us…

This hasn't been easy to write. It has been both traumatic and liberating. I have been trapped in fear for seventeen years. I was told never to tell. Until I turned twenty-three I didn't ever tell. I was filled with too much hate and self-loathing. Telling, writing it down, has set me free. But letting go of fear and shame hurts at first. Pretending it didn't wouldn't be truthful.

My journey to "healed" has not been an instantaneous experience, nor has it finished, but I am learning to love myself. Learning to be kind to myself. I have had to journey through a lot of challenges on this path but it has made me a stronger person. I haven't always felt strong; in fact there've been times when it's felt like I don't have the strength to carry on. Coming to faith has helped me in those times, because I can remember that it's not in my strength that I can do things, but in Christ's. It's not easy to remember that sometimes, and when I fail, it's in those times that I most need to be kind to myself.

Seeing it written down doesn't change the fact that it happened. It does make it seem more real but it's not actually any worse. If anything I can read it back more objectively and find it easier not to blame myself. I can look outside of myself and see a child. Not the adult I am now. It's easy for me to look back and try and put adult responsibilities on a child's shoulders because I am now an adult. When I read it back I'm reminded of the fact that I was, in fact, a child. I could never be responsible for making an adult hurt me.

I don't want my story to be a list of traumas or just pain. That just tends to make abusers seem like giants who can't be defeated. I want my story to show that I came from there and have become something so much more. I have become a child of the King of kings. I am his precious child.

And I have something I've never had before. I have a courage in my heart that hasn't always been there. I asked God to take my fear and shame and I believe He has. I believe He took that and replaced it with courage and a knowledge that it was not my fault.

Tania, your reaction to my story gave me strength. I'm not going to lie... I was terrified that I would be hated for what I shared. But the relief knowing that didn't happen – quite the opposite, you loved me... it's been liberating.

My story

I grew up in a "normal family" but when my parents divorced my life changed forever. When I was nine I began to be abused by my grandparents. I had stayed with them for the first time alone (without my siblings) and I had had the best day of my life: I was treated like a princess and enjoyed being the centre of their attention. Unfortunately, my joy and happiness was not to last. Late that night I woke from a nightmare and sought out the comfort of those familiar people, my grandparents. I climbed into bed seeking comfort, but received something I didn't want: sexual abuse at the hands of my "loving" grandfather. He put his hand up my nightie. He betrayed me. I was so confused. I was so hurt. He took me back to bed. He told me not to tell anyone. But I did. I told Nanna. She washed my mouth out with soap, called me a liar and told me never ever to tell anyone that lie again. She then bathed me and crossed another boundary by cleaning me in a way a Nanna shouldn't. She told me it was what girls did to make sure they were clean.

Following this weekend, my grandparents crossed more and more boundaries with me. I was subject to abuse, from both parties every time I stayed. They progressed from touching to oral sex. I was made to touch them, and I was made to participate in a threesome with them, not intercourse… but touching and other stuff. My grandfather was becoming more and more bold with his actions.

Then Nanna got sick. Really sick. She died from cancer when I was twelve. I was devastated. I loved her. But I was also relieved. I thought I wouldn't have to stay any more. But I did. And so I became his sole source of release. He took my virginity when I was aged twelve. He made me believe it was the way to show I loved him. He brainwashed me into believing it. My body even responded to him, I had been trained very well. None of that changes whose fault it was. None of it means it's my fault. He was an adult. I was a kid. A seriously screwed up, brainwashed and vulnerable kid. I held a lot of guilt over my part in the abuse for a long time, but I don't anymore. But I'll get to that later.

I was made to take part in his sadistic fantasies. He tortured me too, more as time went on. I won't go into the details: it wouldn't be helpful to share that. The things he did to me were awful, beyond anything I could possibly create an analogy for, only to say that he hurt me in every way it is possible to hurt someone. He knew some pretty messed up people who liked little kids. He got me involved in a child pornography ring. He sold me to men and women. I did what I was told. I struggle processing some of the things that happened. I hated myself.

This abuse lasted throughout my teens. When I turned sixteen I got a Saturday job. This limited the amount of time I could go to his. But he still managed to get to me. He always managed though it became less frequent as I reached eighteen due to heading to university. It did not end until I was twenty-one. Unfortunately, the abuse I suffered made me an easy target for other abusers and as such I fell into the hands of many others who were waiting for a victim.

There were a lot of repercussions, other than the obvious, from these sustained levels of abuse. I hated myself so much that I developed an eating disorder, starving myself and then purging whatever food I ate. I cut myself and injured myself in other ways. I was often experiencing suicidal thoughts. This went on for years. The self-harm and eating issues lasted long after the abuse. They became my "normal". My instinctive reaction to failure was self-loathing, and as such I punished myself regularly. I was consumed with it. I hated it but I hated myself more. I wanted to destroy myself. I came pretty close to it a couple of times. I just wanted to be free from the pain. But something always protected me at the right time. Be it a family friend popping round unexpectedly and finding me, or a nursing student friend discovering a passed out girl and acting quickly to save me. The last time I came close I prayed for the first time in a long time. I prayed for God to end my suffering.

And He did.

I had been a member of a support site for abuse victims for a number of months. I was not getting anywhere. But that same day I prayed, I got a response to one of my posts. The person who responded said something to me that restored my hope just a little. She said she had read my post, she had heard me and she wanted to reach out. There are 33,000 members on that forum. First it was just everyday emails, then phone calls, then she invited me for a visit. I know that sounds insane. But I was at rock bottom. I was suffering from insomnia, depression, anxiety, PTSD, flashbacks and trauma memories. All day every day. I had nothing to lose. So I went. She started off as my friend, then became my confidante, and then she took me in. She became my mum. She took me in her arms and showed me what it was to be loved. Real love. Not some twisted version like the one I had grown to know.

My mum is a Christian. She has helped others before, not abused like me, but people who needed to learn what it was to be loved. And after finding her, plus therapy and care, I came to know God's love for me too.

I've come a long way since then. That was fours years ago. I am healing, slowly but surely. I no longer have nightmares, anxiety attacks, and I am beginning to enjoy life. Don't get me wrong, every day I remember what happened to me. Every day I have to cope with the after-effects of the abuse. But also, every day I get to live.

God taught me how to love again. How to be loved. It's a journey that has not been easy. God and I have had our fallings out… or rather I've had my fallings out with Him. But He has always forgiven me. And He is still healing me.

I used to ask… why did You let this happen to me, why didn't You stop it? And I've not got the answers. But I know that He will use this for His glory. In the Bible, when bad people tried to destroy people like Joseph, Daniel, and even Jesus, God turns those things around and uses them for good. I don't know what God has in mind for me, but I know it will be for good.

Bravely, my friend has scribed her own reflections on the benefits of having used kindsight… She writes:

Learning to love myself even when I feel I don't deserve it. Even when I feel like there is no way God could love me because I think I'm too awful. I do deserve it, and God does love me. It isn't always easy to recognize His love, especially when we don't believe we have any value. I believed I was worthless because of the terrible things that were done to me. I believed that any value I had had was gone, tainted and tarnished by my past.

Over time I've been able to look at myself from the outside… as I would see someone else in my position. I wouldn't hate that person! So why should I hate myself? Instead of looking at myself and seeing only dirt and grime… I need to see myself as I was then, a vulnerable child.

God views us with love and care. And if He can look at me like that, then I should too. He values me. I am precious to him. So I need to be precious to me too.

I have a lot of old habits in my brain that automatically push me to negative emotions and views of myself, but with time these are becoming less frequent. There are days when I can actually imagine a time when those habits will be gone for good. That's when I know I'm on the healing journey.

I am not alone and He is with me, no matter how alone I feel. I remind myself that I am loved by good people and by the One who is perfect and pure.

I will never (this side of eternity) know why I had to experience what I did, but knowing wouldn't change it anyway. It's not OK, but it doesn't change that God loves me.

You can heal from hurt. It is possible, even when it feels totally impossible.

You have to learn to forgive yourself and love yourself.

Well, folks. Would you stand with me to applaud this remarkable young lady? I feel both humbled and inspired by her. I count it a privilege along with those other remarkable individuals in her life, such as her adoptive mum, to be able to create spaces for her to express what's inside, be that just listening, or reading accounts articulated for the first time, or just affirming to her how beautiful she is. She is courageous beyond measure.

I'm deeply touched she considered this book a safe and helpful forum for her voice to be heard in regard to the injustice she encountered. May she continue to find peace, joy, and love in abundance. Bless you, girl-friend.

My friend's story highlights the plight of children who've been exploited, some for years, into their adult life. This is a particularly grave injustice, due to the vulnerability of children. They just cannot stand up for themselves, nor defend their voice or body. They need the adults in their life to model goodness, safety, and security. When this is violated, it touches their soul, not just their body. Child sexual, physical, and emotional abuse is damaging beyond belief. Yet, as my friend has shown us, there is hope for those who have suffered; there is a future and a life to be lived, as hard as that may be to believe and trust in. She is proof.

I'm sure there will be a million and one reactions and responses to reading my friend's story, each dependent on our own experiences. Some will react with sheer compassion, some with shock, a few even with indifference, such is the fatigue from life. Some may respond with recognition of elements that echo with their own story. If there's anything you've read that has raised any issues for you, please seek out someone to talk to. If there's no one you feel you can trust, then there are some organizations that will be able to support you. We will list them at the back on a resources page.

As it is with all trauma caused by injustice, whatever our age, it takes trust to believe that life may ever feel right again. Injustice often spins things into disarray and chaos. Having experienced injustice in my own life, I have found its unpredictability hard. I didn't know from one minute to the next what untruths I was going to have to negotiate; what outcomes I just had to suck-up; or what impact was going to be forced on to my children and me. It was really tough. As I found out, oftentimes with injustice, it's not just the pain of personal violation which in itself can be excruciating, but the secondary factors such as loss of control, removal of choice, and lack of being able to take pre-emptive action that are crippling in themselves.

Knowing a bit more keenly how injustice feels now, I have intentionally looked back to assess how I have historically handled situations where others have shared with me when they're going through a miscarriage of justice. It's one thing to work with an organization such as Love146, a cause, a movement – but it's another thing altogether, as with my friend, to hear into the heart and pain of one individual. There's nowhere to run. I've asked myself with kindsight, "How compassionate was I really?"; "Did I feel the extent of their pain or was I just paying lip service to it?"; "Did I deeply listen or offer worn platitudes even if they were in context?" And upon reflection, I feel I've scraped through with a very average "pass".

But seeing as our time together here is about being kind and through that learning, I'm happy to accept I have room to grow in my responses from here onwards.

What I have learned is that it's an easy exercise pontificating the theory of response to injustice and laying forth lazy statements to others that one should "just forgive" or "just let it go". If only it were that easy. And doesn't the word "just" get massively overused! I've noticed it more and more since first noticing! Other regularly used "spiritual" statements I've both given and received are "All we have to do is trust Him" or "All things work together for good for those who love Him" – have you ever had someone say that to you? I have, recently, and while the sentiment of the Scripture is faultless, the use of it isolated me even more due to the nature in which it was bandied about.

Offering out this simplistic "*just* move on" approach, in my experience, belittles the depth of pain, shame, and humiliation that looms large when an injustice is being perpetrated against someone. Let's be honest, even as mature Christians: the majority of us can only imagine having the type of character that is so developed as to be able to handle a serious injustice and smile and say, "I count it all joy!" I've witnessed a situation recently where someone judged another's character as not being "Christ-like" enough, after they had confessed to struggling to cope with a significant injustice against them. The Scripture used against this hurt party, like a new piece of legislation, was Matthew 5:44–45a: "But I say to you, love your enemies, bless those who curse you, do good to those who hate you, and pray for those who spitefully use you and persecute you, that you may be sons of your Father in heaven" (NKJV). Wouldn't we all want to love our enemies! And do good to those who've twisted our insides, and left us with no safety emotionally. And bless those who've brought shame and pain in measures not thought possible. And pray for those who've brought our once secure house to come crashing down!

I want nothing more for us than to have the type of character that could act with such humility and godliness. But it helps no one to use Scripture as a beating stick to measure us against what we're not doing. One small offering of grace towards an "enemy" at times of great pressure is a massive, Herculean act, and can't be dismissed because one isn't staging a twenty-four-hour prayer sit-in accompanied by taking the clothes off our back, ironing them while handing them over with our bank cards to the "enemy".

Kindsight recognizes that, and applauds the acts perhaps not seen, that may not be hugely demonstrative, that perhaps don't go quite far enough for some, but we see as acts of worth and applaud them we will! Because one act of grace or kindness shown, when staring into the bloodshot eyes of injustice or an enemy, is a victory!

I have personally felt the tsunami of hatred towards someone in times past due to how they've treated me. Man, it was ugly. Toxic. And overwhelming. (I'll spare you the details!) They were powerful feelings. I didn't want to feel that way; I wanted to "love my enemy"; I tried and prayed and tried and prayed and tried and prayed. And I had a small sliver of success, but I can't report it was an overnight spiritual success.

If this is your experience too, we must not beat ourselves up about it, rather just keep trying and learning as we go. To have the character, the spiritual fortitude, the level of emotional maturity; to breathe and bless them; to be able to put down the need to defend; to not justify; to refuse to gain one upmanship; to not seek their downfall – that's the stuff of spiritual giants! A worthy, noble, and Christ-like quest indeed. To love, bless, do good towards and pray for an "enemy" is a mind-bendingly hard and spiritually gargantuan task. And as I have learned it is only going to be possible by the power of the Almighty. It certainly won't be in our strength.

Perhaps that's the best place to start. Knowing we cannot do it alone. It's a supernatural thing to do and therefore needs a supernatural God to journey it with us. So we become "naturally super" at the things our frail humanity has little capacity for.

Some Christians struggle with the concept of anger, and feel guilt for feeling it. Personally I feel that anger is a God-given emotion that has a vital role to play in processing emotions healthily. Jesus Himself exhibited anger. We're told in Scripture when Jesus cleared the temple of the money-changers and animal-sellers that He showed great emotion and anger (Matthew 21:12–13; Mark 11:15–18; John 2:13–22). And when the Pharisees refused to answer Jesus' questions, "He looked around at them in anger... deeply distressed at their stubborn hearts" (Mark 3:5, NIV).

It's what we do with the anger that matters. If it leads us and others into creating an energy that brings justice from injustice, or truth from deceit, then it has a place. And as long as it doesn't cause further sin by hurting or disrespecting others, then it's not adding to the issue. Jesus wasn't, it seems, too concerned about damaging property. I'm sure the odd table would have lost a leg or two in his fit of rage. He'd get an ASBO nowadays if He turned over the tables at the local church fete!

What's powerful is the recognition of the emotional stages we will each need to move through if we are to psychologically process the trauma encountered.

There's a necessary pathway to walk down that would normally involve various stages, like

- denial

- anger

- bargaining

- depression and

- acceptance, which includes forgiveness.

Not dissimilar to processing loss or grief. Forgiveness towards others heals us as it separates us from the power of the perpetrator and frees our souls. Bitterness ties us to the perpetrator.

It's also with buckets of kidnsight that we need to recognize that to forgive someone a heinous offence (or even a tiny one!) is **not** to condone it. Every one of us needs to have that truth absorbed into our souls. To forgive is not to condone. To forgive is to be free.

Whether we feel we're winning the battle or not, we can't live in offence, anger, and seething resentment: it's too destructive, regardless of whether we are "entitled to" or not.

We cannot assign to ourselves the same level of disrespect shown to us. This is a death knell to our soul. It simply enlarges the impact of the injustice perpetrated. Instead, we must assign to ourselves greater respect, at the very least for having survived the experience. We have choice as to our response, regardless of what is done to us. We are terrifically capable of making this type of choice. It is in us. We must hold tight on to truth, goodness, and respect. Respecting ourselves, however hard. Respecting ourself is a natural force field that pushes away dark forces. It makes a statement as to our value. It's powerful.

When an injustice has happened, we need to deal with the fallout, often practically, then allow for the emotional consequences to be felt, and give them space. To just try and dump them is self-defeating, because it's like fly-tipping: the chances are someone will turn up on your door serving you with a fine, just when you thought you'd got rid of the stuff!

Only once there's space can we begin to assess the scene, and intuitively identify our way to healing. Sometimes, finding a gifted therapist trained in helping people orientate through complex situations is a really useful aid. They can often help point things out we may not have thought of, or indeed simply reflect our story back to us in a way that provides clarity and objectivity.

All this is very good advice, even if I say so myself, but it takes intentionality. If you're anything like me, it may be that at times you want to run away; think you've dealt with it; find something to distract you; and wonder why, in a few years' time, there's an odd feeling of discomfort on the posterior, otherwise known as "coming back to bite you on the bottom". It's worth putting the effort in now. Not least because life will likely throw other things at us over time, and any accumulation of unprocessed pain will find a way of coming out to be heard. It's much better for ourselves and others if we can face pain head on. It's worth it in the long run. God wants us whole and healed in order to live life to the full.

To all those across the globe dealing with an injustice, may the God of justice walk with us. May He equip us with hearts that heal, hearts that love, and hearts that forgive. This is to be free. Amen.

10

On Learning to Live through Crushing Loss

Loss and bereavement are the only certainties in life. They are sadly utterly inevitable. Not only is every single one of us going to experience loss in some shape or form, but everyone in our life is going to experience loss. And not only is every single one of us going to cease life on earth at some point, but the people in our lives are also going to die at some point.

I shared just that at a Christian conference some years back, and one lady piped up, "Well, that's not very faith-filled!" I asked her why so, to which she replied, "Jesus says by His stripes we are healed, and so I'm believing in that!" And she promptly left. An awkward silence ensued.

Call me a realist but there's real evidence to suggest we all die eventually, and that it's not somehow a lack of faith in Jesus' ability to heal, the fact that we do indeed all perish. I don't know about you, but I don't want to live forever, as I am! At the time of writing, I am forty-one and things are sagging so much that I have no idea what another forty, hey, eighty years would do! As Christians we're promised a new body upon death, no pain, no tears, but a new heaven and a new earth. I'm up for that, Lord! It only takes a few minutes of extrapolation to consider what

would happen if we didn't die but just aged, billions of us...
old – not altogether a fun image, is it?

Now, the real issue is that some people die prematurely, before their time. And yes, in these instances, we look heavenward and passionately petition Jesus for healing. And some people are healed. And goodness, do we thank God when that happens. It's beyond what our minds can comprehend and it reminds us of the power of the God we serve. And sometimes, people aren't physically healed, even though we've prayed and believed for their physical restoration. Such as my mum, my close friend Jay, and the two babies in my womb. We each will have our own stories, of both celebration and desperate sadness.

With kindsight I've allowed myself to admit that it's not always easy for a Christian living with this disconnection: of knowing what God is able to do and loves doing (bringing healing and wholeness to His people), yet we do not always see it outworked, particularly when we find ourselves or our loved ones need healing, and, for whatever reason, it just doesn't happen.

In seeking a way to resolve some of this tension, I talked at length with many friends, thinkers, and theologians. Much was learned, much agreed with and at times disagreed with. My friend Russell Rook said something which has best helped me live in the tension – "God will always save, and sometimes He heals". Simple. But powerful.

We may not always see the type of miraculous physical healing we'd like for ourselves or others, but God assures us of salvation, an eternal and beautiful gift. The ultimate healing in effect.

Now, that... that I can put my faith in. I won't ever stop praying or believing for healing for others or indeed for myself, but I've pinned this on to a much bigger theological notice board now than I used to, and it feels a whole load better, I can tell you. I've got it back in perspective again. When Jesus heals, I now give thanks. When healing doesn't happen in the way I'd like to see, I give thanks salvation is assured and that we are destined to eternal life in paradise with our Father.

I studied at an excellent Bible college that operates with tremendous faith in all regards. I was blessed for having had some brilliant teaching over the years I was there, and I was inspired beyond belief as to how big my God was. I remember having to work hard at understanding that there is no formula we Christians can engage in, in order to receive God's healing or blessing, such as entering into more worship, racking up more fasting days, giving more money, or engaging with more prayer. Our God is not a transactional God in this regard: I'll do this for you, if you do this for me. No, he's a generous, loving, gracious God who desires to pour out huge blessings on us.

Matthew 7 reads:

> *You parents – if your children ask for a loaf of bread, do you give them a stone instead? Or if they ask for a fish, do you give them a snake? Of course not! So if you sinful people know how to give good gifts to your children, how much more will your heavenly Father give good gifts to those who ask him.*[44]

44 Matthew 7:9–11 (NIV).

He hasn't got a list or set of criteria that once I meet the mark it suddenly makes me eligible for "a healing". Quite the opposite. There's only one criterion, and that's that I love Him with all my heart and all my mind. And to ask Him, as a daughter would a loving father, when I am in need.

He wants me to have the most God-fulfilled life, which He's ordained. He has good, good gifts for me that He wants to lavish on us from heaven.

But this doesn't necessarily equate to a trouble-free, suffering-avoidant, financially wealthy life! Which is where some churches have landed their theology.

What if I'm a God-fearing farmer in Ethiopia, living in a perpetual drought, unable to feed my family? Any gospel message still needs to be as true for him as it is for me. The gospel cannot and must not be tailored theologically for the Western experience.

I've noticed across the church, globally, that thankfully we are thinking this stuff through in greater depth and are more prepared as a mature body of Christ to remember that He suffered and suffering is a very real part of our human experience. We live in a fallen world and bad things happen to really good people, as much as good things happen to bad people as we discussed in the very first chapter. In Matthew 5:45 we read, "for He makes His sun rise on the evil and on the good, and sends rain on the just and on the unjust" (NKJV). So, if at any point you have felt that somehow God is not on your side or that you feel perhaps slightly substandard because life isn't great right now, breathe.

And with kindsight know that God *is* on our side and if life isn't a bed of roses, know He's walking it with us. He doesn't reject us, nor forsake us, whatever we've done or not done. Yes, He disciplines those He loves – but forsake us, never. The famous "Footprints in the Sand" poem has ministered to me in this regard on many, many an occasion. Mary Stevenson, the author, expresses that when we feel He has abandoned us, He has in fact been carrying us, which is why there is only one set of footprints in the sand at those points in the picture she paints of our journey through life. Beautiful.

The maturity of our relationship with Jesus is of course tested at times and, speaking from experience, I have most questioned Him when I'm suffering. Loss and suffering can come in all shapes and sizes; it can be short-term, long-term, it can be emotional, spiritual, and of course physical. Whatever its form, it's tough. It can be disheartening, isolating, and cause doubt about faith and life in general to creep in.

A very good friend of mine suffers from serious migraines. She has a busy family life and carries lots of responsibility, both at home and at work. The migraines range from headaches that she can cope with through to pain that causes her to spend hours under the covers in her darkened bedroom. She's had to go to all sorts of migraine clinics, and pain management clinics to try and find a medication that works. Some things worked; some things didn't. It literally affected every area of her life: her confidence, her self-esteem, family life, work. Thankfully her husband is a good, good man, who steps in when needed and is a loving husband and father. But it's gone on for my friend for years. Bless her heart. There have been times when my friend has been so down about the affliction that she's lost a sense of liberty, joy, peace of mind, and her physical strength.

She has shown remarkable courage and determination and I have been inspired by her. She deserves a medal. For perseverance. She never gives up praying for healing, keeps trying to find solutions and ways forward, and is a strong and dynamic women regardless of the pain she lives with. Never a victim, always a successor.

With kindsight I've learned that a loss of capacity in our life, a loss of skills, a loss of physical ability has a massive emotional impact that often we can overlook. Take a moment to perhaps think of a time when your physical health has been affected. Can you recall feelings of helplessness and despair? Did you ever acknowledge the impact that had on you psychologically? Likewise, do we need to offer out some support and grace to someone else who's suffering? Just to acknowledge that someone's suffering can be of great solace to the sufferer.

Likewise, too, the loss of a relationship that doesn't work out can cause immense suffering. It is the passing away of a connection, an ideal of what was to be, a loss of a future construct that we perhaps allowed ourselves to believe in and hold on to. I always take it very seriously, therefore, when in my church or community I hear of a relationship that's not worked out. I know how it feels. I know the gnawing sense of failure, of fear for the future, of loneliness. It's very rare that relationships end mutually beneficially for both partners, so someone is often left in an emotional pickle. This is a loss, a very real bereavement. A very real suffering.

So it is with a change in employment status, perhaps redundancy or getting the boot from a job. There is a societal embarrassment that still pervades this scenario and which is hard to bear. Or perhaps loss of a cherished dream. Whether it's ourselves or of those we know, we all can recall people who've hung on in there for something in particular for a very long time. And it just hasn't materialized. After a while we get embarrassed that it's not happened for them: we smile at them, thinking all the while, "I hope they don't ask me to pray again for them; I haven't got any more nifty one-liners of encouragement." Don't tell me you haven't thought that! The loss of a cherished dream or something that's not come to fulfilment is very difficult and causes much suffering.

Having seen it at close quarters, I have learned about the loss of cognitive capacity. This can be an incredibly stressful, distressing protracted event, for all. My loved, fit, handsome, healthy dad moved in with me a few years back and the plan was to build a granddad-annexe at the back of the garden: a "posh shed" as he called it. There were mutual benefits, inasmuch as I would have the benefit of a babysitter for my two adopted babies, and have somebody around the house who could do the DIY! Being a community-minded person, this filled me with delight.

And then he had a stroke. The stroke has left him with some significant memory loss and reduced capacity for problem-solving and executive functioning. Cooking became a challenge, as did counting money accurately, recalling conversations, people's names, and so on. His driving licence was revoked, taking with it his liberty and freedom to pootle about in the car. In an instant, not only had a dream gone but joyous, practical life experiences were now gone too. And a part of my dad along with them. Six months or so after the stroke he was diagnosed with early-onset Alzheimer's. His illness has been significant for us as a family, and while he's as positive as ever, the adjustments that needed to be made, for us and Dad too, are notable.

Now that we are in this position I've heard so many more stories of people who are trying to care, or coordinate care, for family members with dementia. Some stories are so painful to hear. It can put an incredible strain on a family. Particularly if there are some not-so-helpful relatives in the mix too, who have opinion on a lot but serve very little. Just as there's huge relief when wider family support, dig-in, show love and practical support, as has been our case.

With kindsight I've learned that it's not just about dealing with the illness; it's partly about dealing with the "emotional" loss of the loved individual – because they are in essence different from how we knew them. And that takes adjustment, over and over. Thankfully, what with the outstanding and loyal support of a trusted friend and compassionate carer Dave, and then latterly finding a superb Christian supported-housing flat, equidistant from my sister and me, we are carving out the right solution for us as a family in dealing with this. And Dad himself is a happy, content old boy, so we have much to be thankful for.

And we have to allow ourselves to feel these losses. To feel the suffering. It's not anti-Christian or being without faith to recognize the real consequences and emotional turmoil felt with loss and suffering. It is only by feeling it that we can process it, and by processing it, move on forward, whole.

In my life I have loved a lot of people, and I have lost a lot of people. I have known joy and I've also known intense sadness. As I have mentioned before, my mum passed away several years ago from cancer. I lost money on an Australian property sham. I've experienced redundancy. My nephew died at just twenty-four hours old. One of my closest friends died of breast cancer. I've had two babies die in the womb – heartbeats detected one day, and at the next scan, nothing. They passed away in my body. A good friend and father to one of my godchildren committed suicide. Dad's stroke happened and his dementia was diagnosed six months after adopting both a seven-day-old baby and a thirteen-month-old. A significant relationship I thought would be lifelong, broke down.

It's no wonder I'm asked to speak a lot on loss and bereavement!

My mum was diagnosed with cancer after she went into hospital with kidney stones. Upon starting to operate, they had a look and saw she was just riddled with cancer. They sewed her back up and we got a phone call to come in, where they shared the information that she had six to twelve weeks left to live. She lasted eighteen months but what a traumatic time this was. The reason I mention it in detail is that both she and my dad were strong believers – my dad is still. The were times when, during Mum's illness, Dad would cradle her in his arms like a child, playing soft classical music and burning lavender oil. He would rock her from side to side as she had her head in his chest and he would speak Scriptures over her, Scriptures of healing and well-being, and I would watch, as a daughter, and think if anyone should be healed, it's her: she's a really good woman. And he's a really good man; he needs her. She's loved God the majority of her adult life; she's only fifty-eight; she's got too much left to live; I need her. All these things go through your mind at rapid speed a million times over. But physical healing didn't happen in the way that I wanted it to. As has been the case with all the loved ones I still miss deeply.

With kindsight it's only honest therefore to share that there are days in times past when it was hard to feel settled as so much had been lost. I've had times when I've doubted His goodness and kindness and His desire to heal has been sorely questioned. But these times have proven to be furnaces, where what's been left after my questions and doubts have been burned up are small nuggets of gold, that tell of the irrefutable truth of the living Jesus … It means I am fairly unshakable in my faith now, inasmuch as I'm not reliant on Him to perform in order to make me love Him or follow Him. Rather, belief in Him is just there now: a solid faith, that doesn't require "all that jazz" to stay on the dance floor. I trust Him, because I serve Him, and I serve Him because I trust Him. Joshua 24:15b: "But as for me and my family, we will serve the Lord." And I am, above all, saved with the richest of assurances that I will be with Him for all eternity.

Once that solid soul-agreement was in place with Jesus, I could focus on processing loss well. Kindsight has taught me that there is no right or wrong way of grieving, but that there are healthy and unhealthy ways of processing loss. Dependent on what they are, they will either prolong the trauma and therefore delay our ultimate healing, or they will soothe the trauma and aid our healing.

Honesty too is vital when processing loss. Honesty first and foremost with ourselves, and then secondly honesty with others. The reality is that some people don't want us to be honest about stuff. Loss and bereavement sorts the relational wheat from the chaff in our lives. There'll be those who can't cope with your honesty, and they'll avoid you like the plague. That's fine. Cross them out of the address book. Delete them from your phone. (Read Chapter 8, on choosing comrades!) Then there'll be those who ask but don't really want the answer – that's fine. Mark them down as "card only at Christmas". Then there'll be those who ask and genuinely care. These are friends; mark these down as "card and present at Christmas".

I have realized that there's a swathe of people who feel embarrassed if we're going through some form of loss or trauma. It's simply that they don't know what to do or how to react. They may try and avoid the issue (yes, that happens!) or even be mildly offensive in blanking us (yes, that happens!) or not inviting us to general events (yes, that too happens!).

With kindsight I now understand that for these people, our trauma either reminds them of their own undealt with pain or they are dreading the day they have to face the same challenge of loss and so try to stay unaffected by anything similar for as long as possible. Don't spend time worrying about this segment of people or feeling sadness about what they haven't done. There are more important areas to put our energy into.

It's those whom we've identified we'll give a card and a present to at Christmas that we need to be the most honest with. They are who matter right now. And it's these people whom we need to start being honest with. About how we're coping, or how much we're self-medicating, food, sexual distractions, or alcohol, or having sleepless nights over and over.

And we need to be honest with ourselves when dealing with grief, loss, and suffering. There are no rewards given for those who try to manage it all themselves. I've known people avoid taking anti-depressants because of what people might think. There is no shame in using appropriate medication, you know. I sense in some quarters there's a vague stigma attached to using medicine designed to help aid depression or manage anxiety. Don't be pressured by people, including doctors to either take it, or indeed people trying to convince you not to use it! Kindsight has allowed me to see that good medicine is one of the ways God helps us. Be honest with yourself and those around you about how you're feeling and trust your judgment as to whether you need some temporary, or even permanent, medical assistance.

As part of the honesty commitment, journal. Write things down. Yell things out. Go for long walks. Whatever works for you, but find a mechanism whereby you can talk to yourself in a way that is honest.

The psalms are full of honesty. They record that disappointment is part of human experience. There are many books that we can read throughout Scripture that show us this (Jeremiah or Habakkuk, for example) that show us this. The book of Job always helps me keep things in perspective with all of his trauma and anxiety. Let's face it, it was a lot to contend with: the loss of his wife, family, and livelihood, and boils everywhere! We read him railing against God and God turning it around, reframing the whole thing:

> *Then the Lord answered Job from the whirlwind:*
> *"Who is this that questions my wisdom with such*
> *ignorant words?*
> *Brace yourself like a man,*
> *because I have some questions for you, and you must*
> *answer them.*
>
> *"Where were you when I laid the foundations of the*
> *earth?*
> *Tell me, if you know so much.*
> *Who determined its dimensions*
> *and stretched out the surveying line?*

*"What supports its foundations, and who laid its
cornerstone
as the morning stars sang together
and all the angels shouted for joy?"*

Job 38:1–7

And on God continues, talking about the fragility of ostrich eggs, how amazing the tusks of hippopotamus are, and how the chain coats on crocodiles are such a good design!

God is reminding Job of his infinite power and capacity, and is holding Job to the sole task of loving Him. In Job 42 he says, "I am so sorry God"; "I repent, I will sit in ashes and repent". Some of us will still be railing at God about the disappointment of it all and we haven't come full circle yet. We need to say to God, "Your ways aren't my ways; I just recognize that you are much bigger than I am. You are infinite and I'm finite and I repent and I hand myself back into submission to you". Psalm 31:14–15a reads, "I trust in you, O Lord; I say 'You are my God.' My times are in your hand" (ESV). That's not just the good times – **all** of our times are His.

Our times are in His hands. And that time includes managing loss and bereavement. It still affects us, but it doesn't have to overwhelm us. Loss and bereavement inform who we are, yes, but we have a choice about how much we build it into our identity. I have a choice about how much I allow it to take the best of me. You don't "get over it", rather you adapt and "get on with it". It's so important that we learn this as then we don't have to live in grief as a permanent status of life.

I love the concept that we are but a blip on the scale of eternity. A click of the finger is the equivalent to the span of my life in eternity. My mum's fifty-eight years, my biological babies' zero years – these, on the scale of eternity, are a blip, and sometimes, when going through trauma, it's helpful to remember that **this** isn't it. Life isn't always going to look like this. God has so much more in store for us. This part of the journey is a foretaste, a prequel to the magnificence of how our eternity will look – a new heaven and a new earth. I will bear with dignity that which I'm currently experiencing as a respectful doff of the cap to the Creator, who is more eager than I am to get the eternal show on the road!

We've looked in previous chapters at the cycles of grief. It's worth a final look, as it can really aid people in understanding what to expect, or at least to know what to anticipate:

- denial (this hasn't happened; it can't be true; I refuse to believe this)

- moving through to anger (Why? Who's to blame!)

- bargaining zone (please can I swap the pain; if something changes I'll never do that again; I promise...)

- apathy (depression; feeling as though the days are slow and meaningless; my energy's gone; when can I laugh again without feeling guilty; no appetite; friends are hard to bear; how can people just carry on with life), on to

- God willing, acceptance (I may not be happy with it; I may not have wanted it, but I'm at peace with it). Forgiveness can be arrived at here too.

Another very useful tool I've found is to understand our "grief styles". Kenneth Doka PhD is a grief counsellor and expert in helping people manage loss. He talks of two particular styles:

- Intuitive processing (feelings; waves of emotions that come and then subside; talking it out; it's an expressive style)

- Instrumental processing (expressed through passive or overt anger; thinking rather than feeling; suppressed waves of emotion; tendency to try and fix instead of feel – "I can't fix my son who's ill, but I can mend that fence"; transference of pain from the ethereal to the tangible; exhibiting control of a situation even if it's not the thing that needs fixing).[45]

As well as for ourselves, it's helpful to encourage others who may be struggling to know their grief style. And try to explore it with them. If they're exhibiting grief in a certain way that may not be our style, don't judge them! Allow them their way of processing the grief.

Grief that's expressed well has the potential to strengthen and enrich life. It has mine. I am a different person now to who

45   You can find out more about Doka's research in this interview with Victor Yalom: https://www.psychotherapy.net/interview/grief-counseling-doka.

I was fifteen years ago because of what I've gone through. And I know I'll be a different person with a different set of skills and maturity, hopefully in another fifteen years. I only just feel like I've grown up! But I'm different now. I can't not be. I've been affected by things most people would hate to go through.

In many respects it's made me more able to be compassionate, to think in advance on behalf of people and how they might be affected if loss has occurred. It's made me a better pastor, and I can now approach things with sensitivity and grace.

And it's made me real. I can hold sobbing people and whisper, "I understand. Let me connect because I'm not scared of what you're feeling, even if you are."

Where might you benefit from taking a grief stock-check on your life? Are there any "rooms of the soul" with doors still locked? By that I mean undealt-with, unresolved circumstances, however large or small, that are suspended in time and need unlocking and spring cleaning to give you back emotional and spiritual freedom. Perhaps this is our moment to open up to another and trust we'll hear the words "I'm not scared of what you're feeling, even if you are". My prayer is that we can each find our peace again after loss, that we can each find people to hold us tight during and after it, and that we learn magnificently through it. It's a tough teacher but one of the most profound!

I sincerely hope this has been a blessing to you. For those who have struggled with feeling second class because life seems to have been studded with suffering and loss: know that you are precious and loved beyond measure by the One who holds your life in His hands. God has a purpose for our lives even if we can't see it for ourselves. It is to become more like Him. Our experiences in life can all work toward that purpose. Nothing is lost if we don't let it. Not imploding families, not broken relationships, not grief, nor any form of injustice. Everything counts toward growing into the people He created us to be – if we let it.

And that's kindsight. Not beating ourseves up, but learning through it instead. A much, much kinder approach altogether.

Useful contacts and resources

If you have been affected by any of the issues covered in this book, below are a number of suggestions of organizations who would be only too happy to speak to you and offer you support, along with books and other resources that may be helpful to you.

Emotional support

THE SAMARITANS (UK AND IRELAND)

Support for those who are emotionally distressed.
The Samaritans
Freepost
RSRB-KKBY-CYJK
Chris
PO Box 90
Stirling
FK8 2SA
Helpline UK: 08457 90 90 90
Helpline ROI: 116 123
(Helplines are open 24 hours a day, 365 days a year)
Web: http://www.samaritans.org/
Email: jo@samaritans.org

Support for those who are being or have been abused, and those who care for them

LOVE146 (INTERNATIONAL)

Working internationally to end child trafficking and exploitation through survivor care and prevention.
Web: https://love146.org/
Email: info@love146.org.uk / info@love146.org

CHRISTIAN SURVIVORS (INTERNATIONAL)

An online support network for those who have suffered abuse, rape, and trafficking. Includes links to further helplines and resources in the UK, US, and Australia.
http://www.christiansurvivors.com/

CRIMESTOPPERS (UK)

Tel: 0800 555 111

INTO THE LIGHT (UK)

Christian organization providing support, counselling, information, and resources for those who have been abused, and those who support them.
Into the Light
PO Box 64427
London
W5 9HA
Web: http://www.intothelight.org.uk/index.asp
Email: info@intothelight.org.uk

LIFECENTRE (UK)

Supports survivors of rape and sexual abuse.
Adults' support line: 0844 847 7879
Under 18s tel: 0808 802 0808
Text: 07717 989 022
Web: http://www.lifecentre.uk.com/

THE NATIONAL ASSOCIATION FOR PEOPLE ABUSED IN CHILDHOOD (NAPAC) (UK)

Supports recovery from childhood abuse.
NAPAC
PO Box 63632
London
SW9 1BF
Support line (free from landline and mobile phones): 0808 801 0331
(Lines are open from 10 a.m. to 9 p.m. Monday – Thursday, and from 10 a.m. to 6 p.m. Friday)
Web: http://napac.org.uk
Email: info@napac.org.uk

CHILDHELP (US)

Organization concerned with the prevention and treatment of child abuse.
Tel: 1 800 422 4453
Web: https://www.childhelp.org/hotline/

NATIONAL TRAFFICKING HOTLINE (US)

Tel: 1 888 3737 888

NATIONAL ASSOCIATION OF ADULT SURVIVORS OF CHILD ABUSE (NAASCA) (US)

Child abuse trauma prevention, intervention, and recovery.
Web: http://www.naasca.org/

RAPE, ABUSE & INCEST NATIONAL NETWORK (RAINN) (US)

National anti-sexual assault organization.
National sexual assault hotline: 800 656 4673
Web: https://www.rainn.org/

ADULTS SURVIVING CHILD ABUSE (AUSTRALIA)

An organisation in Australia working with those who have experienced various forms of abuse during childhood.
http://www.asca.org.au/#
Professional Support Line: 1300 657 380
Email: counsellors@asca.org.au

LIFELINE SOUTH AFRICA

This organisation offers a National Counselling line for people to talk through a range of issues.
http://lifelinesa.co.za/
Tl: 0861 322 322

Support for parenting, fostering and adoption

Rob Parsons and Care for the Family, *Getting Your Kids through Church without them Ending up Hating God*, Monarch Books, 2011

CARE FOR THE FAMILY (UK)

A UK charity which aims to promote strong family life and to help those who face family difficulties.
Care for the Family
Garth House
Leon Avenue
Cardiff
CF15 7RG
http://www.careforthefamily.org.uk/
Email: mail@cff.org.uk
Tel: 029 2081 0800

HOME FOR GOOD (UK)

Aiming to make adoption and fostering a significant part of the life and ministry of the church in the UK.
176 Copenhagen Street
London
N1 0ST
Tel: 0300 001 0995
Web: http://www.homeforgood.org.uk
Email: info@homeforgood.org.uk

Support in facing addictions/substance abuse

Below is a list of international residential centres for those who require help with addictions.

BETEL (INTERNATIONAL)

http://betelinternational.org/

MERCY MINISTRIES (UK AND US)

http://www.mercyministries.org/

TEEN CHALLENGE (US)

http://teenchallengeusa.com/

Alcohol management

Allen Carr, *Easy Way to Control Alcohol*, Arcturus Publishing, 2001
Sarah Turner & Lucy Rocca, *The Sober Revolution: Women Calling Time on Wine o'clock*, Sarah Turner and Lucy Rocca, Accent Press, 2013

Marriage

John M. Gottman, *The Seven Principles for Making a Marriage Work*, Harmony, 1999. See also http://www.gottman.com/

CARE FOR THE FAMILY (UK)

A UK charity which aims to promote strong family life and to help those who face family difficulties.
Care for the Family
Garth House
Leon Avenue
Cardiff
CF15 7RG

http://www.careforthefamily.org.uk/
Email: mail@cff.org.uk
Tel: 029 2081 0800

Sexual issues

CHRISTIAN VISION FOR MEN (CVM) (UK)

For resources regarding character development and overcoming pornography.
CVM
The Hub
Unit 2 Dunston Road
Chesterfield
S41 8XA
Tel: 01246 452483 (call for international contact numbers)

THE NAKED TRUTH PROJECT (UK)

Organization offering education and recovery programmes to Naked Truth with the aim of freeing lives from the damaging impact of porn.
11 Baywood Street
Manchester
M9 5XJ
Tel: 0161 637 9949

Email: hello@nakedtruthproject.com

Text credits

Extract p. 49 taken from "Remarriage and Blended Families" by Ron Deal. Copyright © 2008 Ron Deal. Originally published on the Focus on the Family website. Used with permission.

Extract pp. 139–140 taken from "The intimate confessions of a female porn fan" by Nichi Hodgson in *The Telegraph* copyright © 2014, Nichi Hodgson. Reprinted by permission of *The Telegraph*.

Extracts pp. 164, 166 taken from *The Four Loves* by C.S. Lewis, copyright © C.S. Lewis, 1960, renewed 1988 by Arthur Owen Barfield. Reprinted by permission of The C.S. Lewis Company and Houghton Mifflin Harcourt Publishing Company. All rights reserved.

Extract pp. 173–74 taken from "We Walk Together" by Sue C. Boynton in *Heart on My Sleeve*, copyright © 1980 Sue C. Boynton. Reprinted by permission of Whatcom County Historical Society.